OBJECTIVE
KET

Annette Capel   Wendy Sharp   Teacher's Book

CAMBRIDGE
UNIVERSITY PRESS

CAMBRIDGE UNIVERSITY PRESS
Cambridge, New York, Melbourne, Madrid, Cape Town, Singapore, São Paulo

Cambridge University Press
The Edinburgh Building, Cambridge CB2 2RU, UK

www.cambridge.org
Information on this title: www.cambridge.org/9780521541503

First published 2005
3rd printing 2006

Printed in the United Kingdom at the University Press, Cambridge

A catalogue record for this publication is available from the British Library

ISBN-13 978-0-521-54150-3 Teacher's Book
ISBN-10 0-521-54150-6 Teacher's Book

ISBN-13 978-0-521-54149-7 Student's Book
ISBN-10 0-521-54149-2 Student's Book

ISBN-13 978-0-521-54151-0 Cassette Set
ISBN-10 0-521-54151-4 Cassette Set

ISBN-13 978-0-521-54152-7 Audio CD Set
ISBN-10 0-521-54152-2 Audio CD Set

Cover design by Dale Tomlinson

Designed and produced by Kamae Design, Oxford

Contents

Map of Student's Book   4

Contents of the KET
examination   7

Unit 1
Friends   9

Exam folder 1   12

Unit 2
Shopping   13

Exam folder 2   15

Unit 3
Food and drink   16

Writing folder 1   20

Unit 4
The past   21

Units 1–4 Revision   25

Test 1   26

Unit 5
Animals   31

Exam folder 3   33

Unit 6
Leisure and hobbies   35

Exam folder 4   38

Unit 7
Clothes   40

Writing folder 2   42

Unit 8
Entertainment   44

Units 5–8 Revision   47

Test 2   48

Unit 9
Travel   53

Exam folder 5   56

Unit 10
Places and buildings   57

Exam folder 6   60

Unit 11
Sport   61

Writing folder 3   64

Unit 12
The family   65

Units 9–12 Revision   67

Test 3   68

Unit 13
The weather   73

Exam folder 7   76

Unit 14
Books and studying   77

Exam folder 8   80

Unit 15
The world of work   81

Writing folder 4   84

Unit 16
Transport   85

Units 13–16 Revision   88

Test 4   89

Unit 17
Science and technology   94

Exam folder 9   96

Unit 18
Health and well-being   97

Exam folder 10   99

Unit 19
Language and
communication   100

Writing folder 5   103

Unit 20
People   105

Units 17–20 Revision   108

Test 5   109

Key to Grammar folder
exercises   114

Photocopiable activities   116

Sample answer sheets   133

Map of Objective KET Student's Book

TOPIC	EXAM SKILLS	GRAMMAR	VOCABULARY	PRONUNCIATION (P) AND SPELLING (S)
Unit 1 Friends 8–11 1.1 Friends for ever 1.2 Borrow this!	Paper 2 Listening: Part 1	Present simple: *be, have* Questions in the present tense	Adjectives describing feelings Personal possessions	(P) The alphabet
Exam folder 1 12–13	Paper 2 Listening: Part 1			
Unit 2 Shopping 14–17 2.1 For sale 2.2 Shopping from home	Paper 1: Part 1 (Reading) Paper 2 Listening: Part 3	*How much ...?* *How many ...?* *some* and *any*	Shopping and shops	(P) /ɑː/ *car*, /eɪ/ *whale*, /æ/ *apple* (S) Plurals
Exam folder 2 18–19	Paper 1 Reading and Writing: Part 1 (Reading)			
Unit 3 Food and drink 20–23 3.1 Breakfast, lunch and dinner 3.2 Food at festivals	Paper 1: Part 6 (Writing) Paper 2 Listening: Part 5 Paper 1: Part 4 (Reading) Paper 1: Part 9 (Writing)	Present simple Adverbs of frequency Telling the time	Food and drink Celebrations Dates (day and month)	(S) Contractions (P) /ɪ/ *chicken*, /iː/ *cheese*
Writing folder 1 24–25	Paper 1 Reading and Writing: Part 6 (Writing)			
Unit 4 The past 26–29 4.1 A long journey 4.2 A trip to remember	Paper 1: Part 4 (Reading) Paper 2 Listening: Part 5	Past simple Past simple: short answers Past simple + *ago*	Nationalities	(S) Regular verbs in the past simple (P) Regular past simple endings
Units 1–4 Revision 30–31				
Unit 5 Animals 32–35 5.1 A trip to the zoo 5.2 An amazing animal	Paper 2 Listening: Part 3 Paper 1: Part 5 (Reading)	Lists with *and* Conjunctions *and, but, or, because*	Animals Collocations with *do, make, take* and *spend*	(P) List intonation (S) *their, there, they're*
Exam folder 3 36–37	Paper 1 Reading and Writing: Parts 2 and 5 (Reading)			
Unit 6 Leisure and hobbies 38–41 6.1 Theme park fun 6.2 Free time	Paper 3 Speaking: Part 2 Paper 2 Listening: Part 4 Paper 1: Part 3 (Reading) Paper 1: Part 9 (Writing)	Comparative and superlative adjectives Comparative adverbs	Leisure activities Descriptive adjectives and adverbs Telephoning	(S) Comparative and superlative adjectives (P) /ə/ *camera*
Exam folder 4 42–43	Paper 2 Listening: Parts 4 and 5			
Unit 7 Clothes 44–47 7.1 The latest fashion 7.2 Your clothes	Paper 1: Part 4 (Reading) Listening for information Paper 1: Part 3 (Reading)	Simple and continuous tenses	Clothes Adjectives to describe clothes	(S) *-ing* form (P) The last letters of the alphabet: w, x, y, z
Writing folder 2 48–49	Paper 1 Reading and Writing: Part 7 (Writing)			
Unit 8 Entertainment 50–53 8.1 A great movie 8.2 Cool sounds	Paper 1: Part 5 (Reading) Paper 2 Listening: Part 1	Modal verbs 1: *must, had to, may, can, could*	Films, music	(P) Short questions (S) Mistakes with vowels
Units 5–8 Revision 54–55				

TOPIC	EXAM SKILLS	GRAMMAR	VOCABULARY	PRONUNCIATION (P) AND SPELLING (S)
Unit 9 Travel 56–59 9.1 Making holiday plans 9.2 Looking into the future	Listening for information Paper 1: Part 3 (Reading) Paper 1: Part 7 (Writing)	The future with *going to* and *will*	Travel, space	(P) /h/ (S) Words ending in *-y*
Exam folder 5 60–61	Paper 3 Speaking: Parts 1 and 2			
Unit 10 Places and buildings 62–65 10.1 Inside the home 10.2 Famous buildings	Paper 2 Listening: Part 2 Paper 1: Part 2 (Reading)	The passive – present and past simple	Furniture, materials Opposites Buildings	(S) Words ending in *-f* and *-fe* (P) Dates (years)
Exam folder 6 66–67	Paper 1 Reading and Writing: Part 4 (Reading: Right, Wrong, Doesn't say)			
Unit 11 Sport 68–71 11.1 Living for sport 11.2 Keeping fit	Paper 1: Parts 3 and 4 Paper 2 Listening: Part 5 Paper 1: Part 6 (Writing)	Word order in questions Verbs in the *-ing* form	Sport and sports equipment Fitness	(P) /b/ *basketball*, /v/ *volleyball* (S) *gu-*, *qu-*
Writing folder 3 72–73	Paper 1 Reading and Writing: Part 9 (Writing)			
Unit 12 The family 74–77 12.1 Family trees 12.2 Large and small	Paper 2 Listening: Part 3 Paper 1: Part 4 (Reading: Right, Wrong, Doesn't say)	Possessive adjectives and pronouns Subject, object and reflexive pronouns *Everything, something, anything*, etc.	People in a family	(P) /aʊ/ *cow*, /ɔː/ *draw* (S) Words ending in *-le*
Units 9–12 Revision 78–79				
Unit 13 The weather 80–83 13.1 Sun, rain or snow? 13.2 Too much weather!	Paper 2 Listening: Part 2 Paper 1: Part 5 (Reading)	*(Not) as … as* *Enough* and *too*	Weather	(P) Unstressed words with /ə/ (S) *to, too* and *two*
Exam folder 7 84–85	Paper 2 Listening: Part 2			
Unit 14 Books and studying 86–89 14.1 Something good to read 14.2 Learn something new!	Paper 2 Listening: Part 4 Paper 1: Part 3 (Reading)	Position of adjectives *Rather than*	School subjects, education	(P) Silent consonants (S) Words that are often confused
Exam folder 8 90–91	Paper 1 Reading and Writing: Part 3 (Reading)			
Unit 15 The world of work 92–95 15.1 Working hours 15.2 Part-time jobs	Paper 1: Part 4 (Reading: multiple choice) Paper 2 Listening: Part 3	Present perfect *Just* and *yet*	Work, jobs	(S) Words ending in *-er* and *-or* (P) /ð/ *clothes*, /θ/ *thirsty*
Writing folder 4 96–97	Paper 1 Reading and Writing: Part 8 (Writing)			
Unit 16 Transport 98–101 16.1 Journeys 16.2 A day out	Paper 3 Speaking: Part 2 Paper 2 Listening: Part 1	Modal verbs 2: *must, mustn't, don't have to, should, need to, needn't*	Transport Collocations with transport Directions	(P) Weak and strong forms (S) *i* or *e*?
Units 13–16 Revision 102–103				

TOPIC	EXAM SKILLS	GRAMMAR	VOCABULARY	PRONUNCIATION (P) AND SPELLING (S)
Unit 17 Science and technology 104–107 17.1 Techno Star 17.2 Science is great!	Paper 1: Part 5 (Reading) Paper 2 Listening: Part 3	Infinitive of purpose Infinitive with and without *to*	Computers, technology Collocations with *get*, *make*, *watch*, *see*	(P) Contractions (S) Correcting mistakes
Exam folder 9 108–109	Paper 2 Listening: Part 3			
Unit 18 Health and well-being 110–113 18.1 Keeping well! 18.2 A long and happy life	Paper 1: Part 6 (Writing) Paper 1: Parts 3 and 4 (Reading) Paper 2 Listening: Part 5 Paper 1: Part 9 (Writing)	Word order of time phrases First conditional	Parts of the body Health	(P) Linking sounds (S) Words which don't double their last letter
Exam folder 10 114–115	Paper 1 Reading and Writing: Part 4 (Reading: Multiple choice)			
Unit 19 Language and communication 116–119 19.1 Let's communicate! 19.2 Different languages	Paper 2 Listening: Part 2 Paper 1: Part 7 (Writing) Paper 1: Part 5 (Reading)	Prepositions of place Prepositions of time	Letters, emails, etc. Countries, languages, nationalities	(P) Word stress (S) Spellings of the sound /iː/
Writing folder 5 120–121	Paper 1 Reading and Writing: Part 9 (Writing)			
Unit 20 People 122–125 20.1 Famous people 20.2 Lucky people *People*	Paper 1: Part 4 (Reading: multiple choice) Paper 2 Listening: Parts 4 and 5 Paper 3 Speaking: Part 2 Paper 1: Part 6 (Writing)	Review of tenses	Describing people	(P) Sentence stress (S) *ck* or *k*?
Units 17–20 Revision 126–127				
Extra material 128–134				
Grammar folder 135–146				
Vocabulary folder 147–150				
List of irregular verbs 151				
Acknowledgements 152				

Content of the KET examination

The KET examination consists of three papers – Paper 1 Reading and Writing, Paper 2 Listening and Paper 3 Speaking.

There are four grades: Pass with Merit (about 85% of the total marks); Pass (about 70% of the total marks); Narrow Fail (about 5% below the pass mark); Fail. For a Pass with Merit and Pass, the results slip shows the papers in which you did particularly well; for a Narrow Fail and Fail, the results slip shows the papers in which you were weak.

Paper 1 Reading and Writing 1 hour 10 minutes

(50% of the total marks)

There are nine parts in this paper and they are always in the same order. Parts 1–5 test a range of reading skills and Parts 6–9 test basic writing skills. You write all your answers on the answer sheet.

Part	Task Type	Number of Questions	Task Format	Objective Exam folder
Reading Part 1	Matching	5	You match five sentences to eight notices.	EF 2
Reading Part 2	Multiple choice (A, B or C)	5	You choose the right words to complete five sentences.	EF 3
Reading Part 3	Multiple choice (A, B or C) AND	5	You choose the right answer to complete short conversational exchanges.	EF 8
	Matching	5	You choose five answers from eight to complete a conversation.	
Reading Part 4	Right / Wrong / Doesn't say OR	7	You answer seven questions on a text that is up to 230 words long.	EF 6
	Multiple choice (A, B or C)			EF 10
Reading Part 5	Multiple choice (A, B or C)	8	You choose the right words to complete eight spaces in a short text.	EF 3
Writing Part 6	Word completion	5	You decide which words go with five definitions and spell them correctly.	WF 1
Writing Part 7	Open cloze	10	You fill ten spaces in a text such as a postcard with single words, spelled correctly.	WF 2
Writing Part 8	Information transfer	5	You complete a set of notes or a form with information from one or two texts.	WF 4
Writing Part 9	Short message (5 marks)	1	You write a short message, such as a note or postcard (25–35 words), which includes three pieces of information.	WF 3, WF 5

Paper 2 Listening about 30 minutes, including 8 minutes to transfer answers

(25% of the total marks)

There are five parts in this paper and they are always in the same order. You hear each recording twice. You write your answers on the answer sheet at the end of the test.

Part	Task Type	Number of Questions	Task Format	Objective Exam folder
Listening Part 1	Multiple choice (A, B or C)	5	You answer five questions by choosing the correct picture, word or number. There are two speakers in each short conversation.	EF 1
Listening Part 2	Matching	5	You match five questions with eight possible answers. There are two speakers.	EF 7
Listening Part 3	Multiple choice (A, B or C)	5	You answer five questions about a conversation between two speakers.	EF 9
Listening Part 4	Gap fill	5	You complete five spaces in a set of notes. There are two speakers.	EF 4
Listening Part 5	Gap fill	5	You complete five spaces in a set of notes. There is one speaker.	EF 4

Paper 3 Speaking 8–10 minutes for a pair of students

(25% of the total marks)

There are two parts to the test and they are always in the same order. There are two candidates and two examiners. Only one of the examiners asks the questions.

Part	Task Type	Time	Task Format	Objective Exam folder
Speaking Part 1	The examiner asks both candidates some questions.	5–6 minutes	You must give information about yourself.	EF 5
Speaking Part 2	The candidates talk together to find out information.	3–4 minutes	You are given some material to help you ask and answer questions.	EF 5

1 Friends

1.1 Friends for ever

Grammar extra	Present simple *be*, *have*
Pronunciation	The alphabet
Exam skills	Listening Part 1: Short conversations

1.2 Borrow this!

| Grammar | Asking questions |
| Vocabulary | Personal possessions, descriptive adjectives – feelings |

Preparation

Make a copy of the recording script on page 116 for each student. This will be used in 1.1.

1.1 Friends for ever

SB pages 8–9

1 The twelve reasons contain examples of the present simple of the verbs *be* and *have*, which will be revised in the Grammar extra that follows exercise 1. Suggest students read the sentences in pairs or threes and decide together which is the most important reason. Elicit their views. Then give students two minutes to write three more reasons in their groups. Elicit their sentences and write some on the board.

E xtension activity

If students enjoy thinking of further reasons why friends are great, suggest they make a large poster for the classroom wall, displaying their own ideas. They could include pictures from magazines to illustrate their reasons, as on the Student's Book page.

G rammar extra

2 Ask students to complete the verb boxes, looking back at the sentences in exercise 1 if necessary. Point out that the full negative form *I am not*, *I have not*, etc. is also correct, although this is not practised here.

Answers

The verb *be*	**The verb *have***
I am, I'm, I'm not	I have, I've, I haven't
You are, You're, You aren't	You have, You've, You haven't
He/She/It is, He's, She isn't	He/She/It has, He's, She hasn't
We are, We're, We aren't	We have, We've, We haven't
They are, They're, They aren't	They have, They've, They haven't

Pronunciation

3 **KET Speaking Part 1**

Students will have to spell something, such as their surname, in the first part of the Speaking test. They are also tested on their ability to process words that are spelled out in Parts 4 and 5 of the Listening test, where they may have to write down a name, part of an address, etc. This exercise checks whether students are familiar with the whole alphabet, as all the letters are covered in the seven names.

Practise spelling in this way regularly during the course.

Before playing the recording, run through the alphabet with the class, eliciting a letter from each student in turn.

After the recording, point out the use of *double R* in question 4. Two of the same letters or numbers together will be said like this in the KET Listening test.

Recording script and answers

1 THE MATRIX
2 PENELOPE CRUZ
3 BART SIMPSON
4 JUAN CARLOS FERRERO
5 DAVID BECKHAM
6 GWYNETH PALTROW
7 QUENTIN TARANTINO

Listening

4 **KET Listening Part 1**

This listening activity includes further spelling practice and introduces students to short conversations, with an emphasis on questions and answers. The recordings here are slightly slower than those candidates will hear in the exam, to build students' confidence. Note that in

Listening Part 1, students will hear five short conversations, with a maximum of four exchanges in each conversation, with two speakers in each, as here.

Ask students to listen and complete the information. If they are particularly weak in listening, play the recording twice and suggest they don't write anything down the first time they listen.

> **Answers**
> 1 13; play football
> 2 Raquel; every day
> 3 her sister; 13
> 4 Lucky / his dog; to the river

Recording script

1

Maria: OK, Matt, let's start with you. What's your best friend called?

Matt: Er, Jonny, and <u>he's thirteen</u>, the same as me.

Maria: Right, and what do you do together, you know, in your free time?

Matt: That's easy to answer. We <u>play football</u>, as much as possible. We're in the same team, you see.

2

Maria: And Elena, what can you tell me about your best friend?

Elena: Well, her name's Raquel. Shall I spell that? It's <u>R-A-Q-U-E-L</u>.

Maria: Uh huh. And when do you get together? Like, just at weekends?

Elena: Oh no, we're best friends, Maria! I see Raquel <u>every day</u> … in school Monday to Friday, of course, and then we go out at weekends.

3

Maria: Kelly-Anne, I know your best friend is Vicky. And you see her every day?

Kelly-Anne: That's right, because Vicky's <u>my sister</u>.

Maria: Mmm, that's a really special friend. So how old are you, Kelly-Anne?

Kelly-Anne: It's my birthday next week. I'll be fourteen … so I'm <u>thirteen</u> now.

4

Maria: Hi, Tom! Come here so I can ask you some questions. Who's your best friend?

Tom: My best friend … that's difficult. I mean, I've got lots of friends, but a best friend? I'd say it's Lucky, my dog. You spell that <u>L-U-C-K-Y</u>.

Maria: Ah, that's sweet. So where do you go with Lucky? Do you take him for walks?

Tom: Of course, every day! We go <u>to the river</u>. Lucky likes the water!

> **Maria:** Hope he can swim. OK, thanks, all you guys. See you.
> **All:** Bye!

 P hotocopiable recording script activity ⋯⋗ page 116

Hand out copies of the recording script, asking students to fill in the missing words as they listen to the recording again.

> **Answers**
> 1 team
> 2 Monday to Friday
> 3 special
> 4 dog

5 Students will hear Maria asking questions and should write their answers as they listen. Remind them to write short answers, as they won't have time to write much. Pauses between questions have been included on the recording but, if necessary, stop the recording between questions, to give students longer to write their answers.

6 Encourage students to use some of the language given, as this will make their questions and answers sound more natural.

1.2 Borrow this!
SB pages 10–11

1 Check that students understand the two verbs *borrow* and *lend*, explaining the difference if necessary. Then give students two or three minutes to discuss the questions. Elicit students' answers and ask whether they ever have any problems when lending things to friends. Check they understand the meaning of *give back*.

2 Ask students to read the photo story in pairs to find out why Sam is angry at the beginning but not at the end. The story includes examples of different question forms, which will be looked at in the Grammar section.

> **Answers**
> Sam is angry at the beginning because Gary's got his CDs. Sam isn't angry at the end because he hears Gary's father is ill.

Grammar

3 Suggest students read through the story again and underline the eleven examples of questions and suggestions. They can decide in pairs which are *Yes/No* questions, which are *Wh-* questions and which are suggestions. (The suggestion forms *Why don't ...* and *How about ...* are included because of the problems KET students have in using them accurately. Draw students' attention to the fact that *How about ...* is followed by a verb in the *-ing* form.)

Ask students to complete the grammar rules on their own and elicit their answers.

Answers
Completed rules:

Yes/No questions in the present tense
- In questions with **have got**, the verb *have* always comes *at the* beginning of the sentence and *got* comes *after* the subject.
  Example: *Has Gary got your Radiohead CDs?*
- In questions with **be**, the verb also comes *at the beginning* of the sentence.
  Examples: *Are you sad or angry? Is he very ill? Are you free tonight, Sam?*
- In questions with **can**, the verb also comes *at the beginning* of the sentence.
  Example: *Can you text him about my CDs?*
- With **other verbs**, we start the question with *Do* or *Does*. The main verb comes *after* the subject.
  Example: *Do you know about Gary's father?*

Wh- questions in the present tense
- In questions with **be**, **have got** and **can**, the verb comes *after* the question word.
  Examples: *What's wrong, Sam?*
  What can we go and see?
- With **other verbs**, *do* or *does* comes *after* the question word. The subject comes next and the main verb comes after the subject.
  Example: *When do you want them back?*

Suggestions
- You can use *Why don't/doesn't* and *How about* to make suggestions.
  Examples: *Why don't we meet at 7.30 at the cinema?*
  How about sending him a text now?

---

4 The eight sentences are taken from the KET section of the *Cambridge Learner Corpus*. This is a large collection of past exam candidates' scripts, which has been compiled jointly by the University of Cambridge ESOL Examinations and Cambridge University Press. The authors have consulted the *Learner Corpus* extensively in the development of *Objective KET*.

Ask students to correct the questions as necessary and compare their answers with another student.

Answers
1 When *do* you want to come here?
2 Where *are you* now?
3 How about *meeting* me at 7 o'clock?
4 (correct)
5 Why *do* you think it is interesting?
6 (correct)
7 How *can* I get there?
8 Who *does he* like?

---

5 This exercise gives students further practise in forming questions. Encourage them to use a mixture of *Yes/No* questions and *Wh-* questions. Go round listening to each pair, correcting their word order if necessary.

Possible questions
Does Sam want his CDs back?
Has Lisa got a mobile phone?
Can Sam go to the cinema tonight?

Vocabulary

6 The adjectives have all appeared in Unit 1. If time is short, this exercise can be set for homework.

Answers

1 ill	3 free	5 pleased	7 angry
2 special	4 boring	6 sad	8 funny

Activity

Ask students to work with a partner and turn to the questionnaire on page 128 of the Student's Book. Tell them to take turns to ask questions and complete a questionnaire about their partner. Elicit information at the end if there is time.

Exam folder 1

Listening Part 1 Short conversations
SB pages 12–13

Ask students to read the information about this part of the Listening paper. Explain that they will have eight minutes at the end of the test to transfer all their answers to the answer sheet.

Tell students to look at the example of the answer sheet for Part 1 and make sure they know how to fill it in correctly. Marks are often lost because candidates complete the answer sheet incorrectly.

It is useful for students to work with recording scripts, especially at the beginning of a course, as this builds their confidence and allows them to understand how each part of the Listening test is structured.

Ask students to follow the procedure as they read the example recording script. Elicit the correct answer (A).

Refer students to the Exam advice box and give them a couple of minutes to read and discuss it. Then ask them to follow the same procedure as they do the exam task.

Answers				
1 C	2 A	3 A	4 B	5 C

Recording script

You will hear five short conversations.
You will hear each conversation twice.
There is one question for each conversation.
For questions 1–5, put a tick under the right answer.

1   What is the man buying for his lunch?
Woman: Can I help you, Mr Stoker? Some soup to take away, as usual?
Man: Not today, thanks. But I'd like something hot – <u>a slice of that pizza</u>, please.
Woman: OK. Anything else?
Man: Just a packet of egg sandwiches for Mrs Brown. I said I'd take some back for her.

Now listen again.
(The recording is repeated.)

2   When is Maria's party?
Woman: David, you know it's my birthday on Friday. Are you free to come to my party?
Man: Oh dear, Maria, I'm in London that day. Can I take you to a restaurant on Saturday instead?
Woman: That's a great idea, and you can still come to my party because <u>it's on Wednesday</u>. It starts at eight thirty.
Man: Great!

Now listen again.
(The recording is repeated.)

3   Which postcard does the woman choose?
Boy: Are you getting a postcard for your sister? Here's a beautiful one of the lake.
Woman: But we didn't go there. I only send cards of places I know. This one of the city at night looks good.
Boy: I agree, but your sister doesn't like cities!
Woman: You're right, <u>I'll get her the forest one</u>. We went there two days ago, remember?

Now listen again.
(The recording is repeated.)

4   How much does the woman pay for the DVD?
Woman: I want to buy a Harry Potter film on DVD. Have you got any under ten pounds?
Man: I'm sorry, no. The new one's nineteen pounds fifty, and that's not a bad price. How about buying the one before that? <u>That's only ten pounds fifty</u>.
Woman: <u>OK, I'll take that one</u>. Here's twenty pounds.
Man: Thank you, and that's nine pounds fifty back. Enjoy it.

Now listen again.
(The recording is repeated.)

5   What did the girl leave at Ben's flat?
Girl: Hello, Ben. Thanks for coffee this afternoon. <u>I think the lights for my bike are on your kitchen table</u>. I put them down there when you gave me my jacket, remember?
Ben: They are. I found them next to my books just now.
Girl: Sorry. Can you bring them to college tomorrow, please?
Ben: No problem.

Now listen again.
(The recording is repeated.)

2 Shopping

<table>
<tr><td colspan="2">2.1 For sale</td></tr>
<tr><td>Vocabulary</td><td>Shops and items you buy in them</td></tr>
<tr><td>Grammar extra</td><td>Questions with countable and uncountable nouns</td></tr>
<tr><td>Exam skills</td><td>Reading Part 1: Matching</td></tr>
<tr><td>Pronunciation</td><td>Vowel sounds /ɑː/, /eɪ/, /æ/</td></tr>
<tr><td colspan="2">2.2 Shopping from home</td></tr>
<tr><td>Exam skills</td><td>Listening (and Reading) Part 3</td></tr>
<tr><td>Grammar</td><td>Some and any</td></tr>
<tr><td>Spelling</td><td>Plurals</td></tr>
<tr><td colspan="2">Preparation</td></tr>
<tr><td colspan="2">For the Extension activity in Lesson 2.2 make copies of the Number Bingo cards on page 117, enough for each student to have one card, and cut them up.</td></tr>
</table>

2.1 For sale

SB pages 14–15

Vocabulary

1 Ask students to spend two minutes on this warm-up activity. Elicit which goods are sold in each place.

> **Answers**
> *bookshop:* book, CD, DVD, map
> *chemist:* aspirin, plasters, shampoo, toothpaste
> *department store:* belt, camera, sunglasses, sweater, umbrella
> *market:* carrots, fish, potatoes, tomatoes, cheese, apples
> *newsagent:* chocolate, magazine, newspaper, sweets

2 Encourage students to write down new vocabulary in meaningful lists. If they don't already keep a vocabulary notebook, suggest this would be useful. They could organise it according to the unit topics in the Student's Book, which represent the topics in the KET examination.

3 Elicit answers to these questions yourself. Then refer students to the Grammar extra box to consolidate the difference between *How much* and *How many*.

Grammar extra

4 Ask students to ask and answer in pairs.

Reading

5 **KET Reading Part 1**

Ask students to look through the notices quickly without reading them and suggest where each notice might be found.

> **Answers**
> **A** on (wool or silk) clothing, e.g. a sweater or dress
> **B** in a supermarket car park
> **C** on a shoe box
> **D** on a menu / at a restaurant
> **E** on a market stall / in a shop
> **F** on a poster/wall/door
> **G** in a shop window
> **H** in a newspaper

6 This is a training activity for the Reading Part 1 matching task, which also revises alphabet use. Because part of each text is missing, students must read the notices very carefully and think about their content. Give students five minutes to write down the missing letters. Then elicit answers, asking students to spell out the letters. Write the full words on the board.

> **Answers**
> **A** HA
> **B** PA
> **C** MA
> **D** PA; SA
> **E** CA
> **F** SA; TI
> **G** CA; SA
> **H** AD; GA; ON; PH

7

> **Answers**
> **1** G   **2** D   **3** H   **4** B   **5** A

Pronunciation

8 These vowel sounds /ɑː/ as in *car*, /eɪ/ as in *whale* and /æ/ as in *apple* are sometimes confused. The sounds are shown here with pictures to help students remember them. Students have already seen most of the words, but check understanding before they listen. Ask students to listen and repeat each word, and underline the relevant sound each time.

Answers

/ɑː/
car
supermarket
artist
department store

/eɪ/
whale
sale
PlayStation
email

/æ/
apple
map
carrot
advert

9 Ask students to look back at the notices in exercise 6 to find more words with the same sounds. Some of the words are those with missing letters.

Answers

/ɑː/	half, parking
/eɪ/	made, games, eight
/æ/	hand, cameras, pasta, salad, and, Saturday

2.2 Shopping from home
SB pages 16–17

1 Give students two minutes to discuss the different ways of shopping: ordering by phone from a catalogue, buying on the internet, looking at magazine adverts in order to select what to buy. Then elicit answers. Suggest reasons for and against shopping from home if necessary.
(*For* – it saves time and can be cheaper; *against* – it is less fun and you can't see the goods you're buying.)

Listening

2 **KET Listening (and Reading) Part 3**

This training activity supports students by presenting most of the recording script on the page and allowing them to predict what they will hear. The answers are confined to numbers and prices. Note that the printed conversation takes the form of a Reading Part 3 task, where candidates have to match responses.

Ask students to tell you what the conversation is about.

Answer
Ordering goods from a swimwear catalogue

3 Play the recording and ask students to listen and fill in the missing numbers.

Answers

1 14 **2** (£)26.40 **3** 77 **4** (£)9.50 **5** 39

Recording script

Kevin: Good morning. Swimshop, Kevin speaking. How can I help you?

Sally: Hello. I've got your catalogue here and I'd like some information. Can you give me some prices?

Kevin: Of course. Please tell me the page number you're looking at.

Sally: OK. The first thing is on page 14 and it's the Maru swimming costume, the blue and green one.

Kevin: OK, the small and medium sizes are £22.65 and the large one is £26.40.

Sally: Right. I'd like to order that, please, size small.

Kevin: Fine. Have you got any more things to order?

Sally: Yes, I'd like some pool shoes for water sports. They're on page 77. How much are the blue and yellow ones?

Kevin: Well, they were £16.50 but they're in the sale now and they're only £9.50. But we don't have any left in small sizes. What shoe size are you?

Sally: I'm a 39.

Kevin: Let me check. Yes, we've got a pair in that size.

Sally: Great. Well, that's all I need. My name and address is …

Extension activity

If students seem weak on their numbers, play *Number Bingo* with them. To do this, you will need to prepare a set of cards from the photocopiable material on page 117. The activity covers the numbers 1 to 50 and there are eight different cards. (Make sure students sitting together do not get the same card.) Hand out one card to each student or, in large classes, ask students to work in pairs. Students should tick any numbers on their cards that they hear you say. The first student to complete a card shouts 'Bingo'. Ask that student to read out the numbers ticked as a check.

Grammar

4 Ask students to read sentences 1–5 and complete rules a–e. Elicit answers to the matching task.

Answers
a some – sentence 2
b any – sentence 4
c some – sentence 1
d some – sentence 5
e any – sentence 3

5 Ask students to complete sentences 1–10 on their own and then compare answers.

Answers
2 some
3 any
4 some
5 some
6 some
7 any
8 some
9 any; some
10 some

S pelling spot

Ask students to read the information carefully. Then ask them to close their books and elicit plural forms for the following words: *potato*, *foot*, *sandwich*, *woman*, *dish*, *story*. Students should spell out these plurals or come up and write them on the board.

Activity

Explain that the activity practises plural spellings. Students can work in pairs.

Answers
ca<u>t</u>, cats
toothpas<u>te</u>
bo<u>x</u>, boxes
foo<u>t</u>, feet
fil<u>m</u>, films
fl<u>y</u>, flies
ma<u>p</u>, maps
camer<u>a</u>, cameras
glas<u>s</u>, glasses
bu<u>s</u>, buses
windo<u>w</u>, windows
tomat<u>o</u>, tomatoes
newspape<u>r</u>, newpapers
han<u>d</u>, hands

The three words say TEXT MY PASSWORD.

Exam folder 2

Reading Part 1   Notices

SB pages 18–19

Ask students to read the information about this part of the Reading and Writing paper.

1 This task shows students some of the key areas of language that are tested in this part of the Reading paper. Elicit further examples for each one.

Possible answers
1 You should   3 Keep quiet   5 in the field
2 bigger   4 at 6.30

2 Suggest students look for examples of the language areas above in the exam task in pairs.

Answers
1 (modal verbs)
   Question 4: You can
   Question 5: You may

2 (comparison)
   Question 1: later
   Question 2: cheaper
   Question 3: lower
   Question 5: younger
   Notice H: longer

3 (imperatives)
   Example 0: Do not leave
   Notice A: Buy
   Notice D: Please put
   Notice G: Spend

4 (prepositions with times/days)
   Notice C: from 7 pm
   Notice E: until then (next Tuesday)

5 (prepositions with places)
   Example 0: on the floor
   Notice A: at machine
   Notice D: above your seat

Refer students to the Exam advice box and make sure they understand the advice given. Ask them to follow this procedure as they do the exam task. Also draw their attention to the example of the candidate answer sheet and make sure they know how to fill it in correctly.

Part 1

Allow students a maximum of six minutes to complete the task.

Answers
1 H   2 B   3 E   4 A   5 F

③ Food and drink

3.1 Breakfast, lunch and dinner

Vocabulary	Food and drink
Pronunciation	/ɪ/ as in *chicken*; /iː/ as in *cheese*
Exam skills	Writing Part 6: Spelling
	Listening Part 5: Note taking
	Listening for detail
Grammar	Present simple
	Telling the time
Spelling	Contractions

3.2 Food at festivals

Exam skills	Reading Part 4: Right, Wrong, Doesn't say
	Writing Part 9: Writing a note
Grammar extra	Adverbs of frequency
Vocabulary	Celebrations
	Dates (day and month)

Preparation

Make one copy of the *UK Fact sheet* on page 118 for each student for the Extension activity in 3.2.

3.1 Breakfast, lunch and dinner

SB pages 20–21

1 | KET Writing Part 6 |

KET Writing Part 6 tests the spelling of lexical items. In the exam, there are five dictionary-type definitions and students need to identify and then spell the item. In this unit there is some preliminary work for this part of the exam.

Ask students to work in pairs. They should talk about the photos and tell each other what they can see.

Ask individual students to come up and write on the board one item of food or drink they can see in the photos. The class should say if the student has spelled the word correctly.

Answers
apples, grapes, bananas, oranges
tomatoes, carrots, onions, salad
pizza, sandwiches, burger, soup
potatoes, rice, pasta, bread
ice cream, cake, biscuits, chocolate
lemonade, orange juice, mineral water, coffee
steak, chicken, fish, cheese

Give the class time to write down the words in their vocabulary books.

Students should then close their vocabulary books and do the word puzzle. This can be done in class or for homework.

Answers
grapes
apple
fish
tomato
chocolate
burger
orange
salad
sandwich
steak

The word in the yellow squares is *restaurant*.

Ask students to look at the photos of the different food groups. Invite them to say why the foods are in those particular groups, i.e. what the foods in each group have in common.

Suggested answers
fruit
vegetables
lunch items / snacks / fast food
carbohydrates / filling foods
dessert/sweet/sugary food
drinks
food containing protein (meat, fish, cheese)

Extension activity

To extend vocabulary, ask: *In the photos, what is the item of food or drink in/on?*

Put the names of other containers (*box, can/tin, jug, glass, packet, jar*) on the board and ask the class, either in pairs or groups, to write down what they think they would find in the containers. This can be done as a game (the first pair or group to finish, with correct answers, are the winners), for homework or just as a vocabulary extension in class.

Possible answers
a box of cereal, chocolates
a can of lemonade
a tin/can of tomatoes
a jug of milk, water
a glass of wine, juice
a packet of soup, sweets, biscuits
a jar of coffee, jam

Pronunciation

2 The focus is on the sounds /ɪ/ as in *chicken* and /iː/ as in *cheese*. Draw students' attention to the pictures. Ask students to repeat each word after the recording. Then ask them to form pairs. Each pair should draw two columns on a piece of paper. They should decide which column each word goes in. Play the recording when they have finished so they can check their answers.

Answers

group 1	group 2
chicken	cheese
fish	meal
fill	leave
biscuit	meat
bin	tea
chips	eat
dinner	feel
sit	seat
live	beans

You could do some spelling practice by asking students to write down the words you say. Choose five words from each column and mix them up. Say each word once and ask them to write it down.

Listening

3 Ask students to look at the photo and the exercise. They are going to hear a boy called Jack and a girl called Katie talking about food and drink. The class should read through the questions. Check that they understand the vocabulary. Explain that you will play the recording twice. The first time they should just listen and the second time they should write down J for Jack or K for Katie next to each question. There is one question where both J and K are needed.

Answers
1 J   **2** K   **3** K   **4** J   **5** J   **6** K   **7** J and K   **8** K

Recording script

Katie: Hi, Jack! Come and have lunch with me! I'm really hungry today.
Jack: Hi, Katie! So am I. I have lots for breakfast every morning but I still eat a lot at lunchtime. What about you, what do you usually have for breakfast?
Katie: Nothing much. I always get a cake or something on my way to school so I don't feel hungry during lessons.
Jack: And then you have chips or pizza for lunch?
Katie: Yes, nearly every day. I like that.
Jack: They're not very good for you, are they? I try to eat a lot of salad. It's healthy. And I drink lots of water. It's better for you than juice.
Katie: I don't like salad very much, and I think tea and coffee taste horrible. I prefer cola or lemonade.
Jack: I bet you like chocolate as well, don't you? I love chocolate.
Katie: Mmm, I love it too, and sweets and biscuits. But I don't like ice cream very much. It makes my teeth too cold!

Vocabulary

4 Write on the board:

I like .... best. / I prefer ....

I quite like ....

.... is/are OK.

I don't like ....

I hate ....

Choose a food item to complete each sentence and write them in a column on the board, in random order, so that the class can't tell which sentence they belong with. Then ask students to guess which of your food items goes in which sentence.

Ask the class to work in pairs, telling each other what they think about each item of food or drink.

5 Students should take a piece of paper and walk around the class to find out what four people like or don't like. Alternatively the class can do this in groups of four, with one person from each group reporting to the class the group's likes and dislikes.

Grammar

6 Students should complete the table with the correct forms of the present simple. Refer students to the section in the Grammar folder on page 136 if they need extra help. The exercise in the Grammar folder can be done in class or for homework.

Answers	
affirmative	I/You/We/They like
	He/She/It likes
negative	I/You/We/They don't like
	He/She/It doesn't like
question	Do I/you/we/they like
	Does he/she/it like

7 KET Reading Part 3 tests functional language such as telling the time, greetings, polite requests, giving opinions, etc. Students read and identify the correct response to a sentence. This exercise introduces telling the time.

Answers					
1 c	2 f	3 a	4 d	5 e	6 b

8 Students should work in pairs to decide which answers are correct.

Answers
A, D, E and F are correct.

Try to elicit why the other answers are wrong and when you could use them. Some examples:
B *Do you play tennis?*
Do you like bananas?
C *Let's go to the cinema.*
Can I have lunch?
G *Have you got a pen?*
Where are you going for your holidays?

S pelling spot

9

Answers
hasn't
haven't
isn't
aren't

10 KET Listening Part 5

KET Listening Part 5 tests the ability to listen to a monologue containing information – spelling of names, places, times, etc. – and write down the missing information.

Elicit from the class the times when they normally eat their main meals.

B ackground information

People in Britain usually have breakfast between 7 and 8 o'clock. Breakfast in Britain is usually toast or cereal. British people rarely eat a full cooked breakfast of sausage, bacon, tomatoes, mushrooms and eggs nowadays, except perhaps at weekends.
Lunch is between 12.30 and 1.30. It is often a sandwich or salad, but may be something cooked.
Dinner is from 6.30 to 8.00. It is often meat or fish with potatoes and other vegetables.

Ask students to read through the table. Check they understand the vocabulary. Tell them they will hear a woman talking about her day and they should fill the spaces with the missing word or words. Play the recording once to get a general understanding and then again so students can write/check their answers.

Finally, ask students to work in pairs and tell each other about their mealtimes.

Answers
1 orange juice
2 1.15 / one fifteen / a quarter past one
3 water
4 6.30 / six thirty / half past six
5 fish
6 (a cup of) coffee

Recording script

What do I usually eat and drink? Well, I get up about seven thirty, have a shower and then have breakfast about eight o'clock. I make a cup of tea, and I have <u>orange juice</u> and then toast. Then, I go to my office – I work in advertising. I don't eat snacks, so I'm quite hungry by lunchtime. I have lunch at <u>one fifteen</u>. I have about an hour for lunch, and I often go to a café near my office. I have salad and I sometimes have a cake – the café does yummy chocolate cakes. And to drink? Well, <u>water</u>. I don't like to have too much tea or coffee in the day.

I get home from work about five thirty. I have my evening meal at about <u>six thirty</u> and I like cooking so I try to make something healthy and interesting – usually chicken or <u>fish</u> with rice or pasta. I never have a dessert, but I do have a cup of coffee after dinner. Then, I often go out – maybe to the cinema or with friends. I'm usually in bed by ten thirty during the week.

3.2 Food at festivals

SB pages 22–23

B ackground information

Buñol is a town near Valencia in Spain. Every year, on the last Wednesday in August, there is a festival, when people come to throw tomatoes at each other. The festival began in 1945, probably as a joke. The festival has continued off and on until the present day. Some years it was banned by the town council as it became more of a riot than a festival, but it has become so popular that now it happens every year. The festival is highly organised and regulated.

1 Invite students to look at, and comment on, the photograph of the Tomato Festival in Buñol. Possible questions:
What are the people doing?
Why are they doing it?
Would you like to be there? Why? / Why not?
Do you know of other festivals like this one?

Reading

2 **KET Reading Part 4**

Ask students to read the text and try to answer the questions. Tell them not to worry about words they don't know at this stage. They should underline in pencil the word or phrase which they think gives the answer. Students should then discuss their answers to the questions in pairs. Check to make sure they understand the vocabulary.

Answers			
1 Wrong	3 Right	5 Wrong	7 Wrong
2 Wrong	4 Wrong	6 Wrong	8 Right

G rammar extra

3 Students should read through the explanation and do the exercise.

Answers
2 My mother usually makes cakes on Tuesdays.
3 I am always hungry at lunch time.
4 I am often late for dinner.
5 Pete always has a party on his birthday.
6 We sometimes have fireworks on New Year's Eve.
7 Sam usually meets his friends on New Year's Eve.
8 You never eat spaghetti with a knife.

Reading

4 Akiko Imai is a Japanese girl. First of all, ask students to read the text to get a general idea of what it is about. Check that they understand the vocabulary. Ask them to do the exercise.

Answers		
2 go	8 listens	14 make
3 doesn't … go	9 rings	15 do
4 stays	10 drink	16 sends
5 begins	11 eat	17 enjoys
6 watches	12 receive	18 doesn't go
7 eats	13 clean	

5 Ask students to work in pairs or groups to discuss what they do on their special days. Put new vocabulary on the board. Check that they are using adverbs of frequency correctly and that they remember to put an *-s/-es* on the end of third person singular verbs in the present simple.

E xtension activity

Explain that students are going to talk about differences between the UK and their own country. Give each student a fact sheet about the UK (see page 118). They then have to discuss what differences there are between their country and the UK. One person in each group writes down the differences. At the end, each group feeds back to the rest of the class.

6 **KET Writing Part 9**

There are five marks for Writing Part 9 in the examination. Candidates are not expected to write perfect English. However, they must communicate all three parts of the message. Do not treat this as an exam task, but encourage students to mention all three points in their answer.

Sample answer

Dear Maria,

We have a special festival in our town on 14th July for Independence Day. We have fireworks in the evening and we have wonderful cakes and sweet biscuits.

Love,
Paula

Activity

Encourage students to use the following language:

- *When were you born?*
- *What's/When's your birthday?*
- *Were you born in November? What date?*
- *My birthday is 12th December.*

Writing folder 1

Writing Part 6   Spelling words

SB pages 24–25

Ask students to read the information about this part of the Reading and Writing paper. It is important to give them plenty of practice in spelling to prepare them for this part of the exam.

Extension activity

Play a game to help students with their spelling. One person thinks of a word and puts dashes for each letter on the board. The class have to guess the missing letters. If they guess wrong, then a line is drawn to form a cat: (1st wrong letter – draw the head, 2nd – an ear, 3rd – another ear, 4th – the body, 5th – a paw, 6th – another paw, 7th – the tail, and finally six whiskers (one wrong letter each). The winner is the first person to guess the word. If nobody guesses the word before the cat is complete, the person who thought of the word is the winner.

1 When the students have finished this matching task, you could ask them to write a similar list of beginnings and endings of words for their partner to do.

> **Answers**
> **2** butter **4** dish **6** market **8** tomato **10** apple
> **3** waitress **5** juice **7** pasta **9** carrot

2 Ask the students to work through the exercise in pairs and decide which word is spelled wrongly. They may use an English–English dictionary to help them.

> **Answers**
> **2** pilot **5** uncle **8** sunny **11** believe
> **3** yellow **6** beautiful **9** which **12** apartment
> **4** mirror **7** telephone **10** comfortable

3 This exercise practises definitions.

> **Possible answers**
> **2** This food is very popular in Italy.
> **3** I will bring you your food in a restaurant.
> **4** This is where you can go to eat lunch.
> **5** This is the first meal of the day.
> **6** This is something small you can eat between meals.
> **7** This is where you cook food.
> **8** This keeps food cold.
> **9** An apple is an example of this.
> **10** This is good to eat on a hot day.

4 The students should spend some time either in class or for homework writing their own definitions for their partner to guess.

Students should read through the Exam advice carefully. Check they understand each point. Care needs to be taken as some answers could be plural. Get students into the habit of checking to see whether the answer will be plural before they do the exercise.

Next to the Exam advice there is an example of an answer sheet. Make sure the students know how to fill it in. Marks are often lost because the answer sheet is wrongly completed.

Part 6

> **Answers**
> **1** lemonade **3** orange **5** sandwiches
> **2** tomatoes **4** sugar

4 The past

4.1 A long journey

Exam skills	Reading Part 4: Right, Wrong, Doesn't say
Grammar	Past simple – regular and irregular verbs
Spelling	Regular verbs in the past simple
Pronunciation	Regular past simple endings: /t/ – *talked*; /d/ – *lived*; /ɪd/ – *decided*

4.2 A trip to remember

Exam skills	Listening Part 5: Note taking
Grammar	Past simple: short answers
Grammar extra	Past simple + *ago*

Preparation

Make one copy of the recording script on page 119 for each student. This will be used in 4.2.

4.1   A long journey
SB pages 26–27

1 Introduce the idea of nationality. Ask students what their nationality is, and exemplify with some famous people the students will be familiar with – footballers, singers, film stars, etc.

Students should go through exercise 1 matching the people with their nationality.

> **Answers**
>
> | | |
> |---|---|
> | Roald Amundsen | Norwegian |
> | Ferdinand Magellan | Portuguese |
> | Ranulph Fiennes (/faɪnz/) | English |
> | Neil Armstrong | American |
> | Hernán Cortés | Spanish |
> | Marco Polo | Italian |
>
> They are all explorers.

B ackground information

Roald Amundsen 1872–1928
Norwegian explorer. His Antarctic expedition of 1910 reached the South Pole in 1911.

Ferdinand Magellan 1480–1521
Portuguese explorer. First circumnavigation of the world. Born in Portugal near Villa Real. Died in the Phillipines but his ship continued back to Spain.

Sir Ranulph Fiennes 1944 –
Sir Ranulph Twisleton-Wykeham-Fiennes. Born in Britain. His 1982 Transglobe expedition was the first to complete a circumpolar navigation of the Earth, i.e. go round the world from Pole to Pole. In 2003 he ran seven marathons on seven continents in seven days.

Neil Armstrong 1930 –
US astronaut. In 1969 he became the first person to set foot on the Moon.

Hernán Cortés/Cortez 1485–1547
Spanish conqueror of Mexico. Born at Medellin. Conquered the Aztecs.

Marco Polo – see below.

Ask students to close their books. Get them to tell their partner everything they know about Marco Polo.

> **Possible answers**
> Marco Polo 1254–1324, famous for his travels in Asia and especially China. Born in Venice. Travelled to China and became a Governor of Yanzhou. Wrote *The Travels of Marco Polo*.

Reading

2 **KET Reading Part 4**

Reading Part 4 can be either a *Right, Wrong, Doesn't say* or a multiple-choice task. The questions are always given in the same order as the information occurs in the text. The best way for students to tackle a *Right, Wrong, Doesn't say* task is to go through the questions, answering 'Right' or 'Wrong' where they can, and underlining the part of the text that tells them the answer. They should then go back through the remaining questions and check that there is no information in the text to answer them, in which case they answer 'Doesn't say'. Stress to students that they should *not* use their own knowledge to answer the questions. For 'Right' and 'Wrong' answers the information *must* be found in the text, and if not, the answer has to be 'Doesn't say'.

Answers
1 Wrong – No he didn't. He went to China when he was 17.
2 Right
3 Right
4 Right
5 Doesn't say
6 Wrong – Kinsai had ten markets.
7 Doesn't say
8 Doesn't say

Grammar

3 This should be revision of the past simple tense. If students require more practice, they should look in the Grammar folder on page 137. There is an additional exercise on that page that they can do in class or for homework.

Answers
1 lived
2 travelled
3 bought
4 sold
5 was/were

Where did the Polo family come from?
Many people didn't believe Marco's stories at first.

S pelling spot

4 First, go through the explanation with students and check they understand the rules.

Answers

1 arrived	5 used	8 played
2 stopped	6 returned	9 carried
3 helped	7 liked	10 opened
4 looked		

Pronunciation

5 The focus is on the sounds /t/ as in *tent* and /d/ as in *dolphin*. Draw students' attention to the pictures. These are the sounds that are made in the regular past simple verb endings.
Students should underline the regular verbs in the past simple. They should then work in pairs and decide how the ending of each verb is pronounced. It might be a good idea to do a few for practice first. For example:
/t/   *talked*
/d/   *lived*
/ɪd/   *decided*

When students have completed the exercise, they should listen to the recording to check their answers.

Recording script and answers

/t/	/d/	/ɪd/
talked	lived	decided
asked	travelled	visited
liked	returned	wanted
	used	
	arrived	
	called	
	stayed	
	believed	
	died	

6 Explain that not all verbs are regular. For a list of irregular verbs, see page 151 of the Student's Book.

Answers

1 wore	5 met	8 went
2 gave	6 took	9 bought
3 ate	7 said	10 saw
4 sold		

E xtension activity

Students should form groups of three. One person should think of something good or bad that really happened to them and then tell the story to the others. They should divide the story into three and each remember one part of the story. They each pretend the story happened to them. They then tell the rest of the class the story and the class has to guess whose story it really is.

Activity

The class should listen to the recording and then try to guess who the person is. They should then play the game themselves, possibly first as a class and then in small groups. They should ask a maximum of 12 to 15 questions.

Recording script

Boy: Are you ready to play?
Girl: Yes, I'm ready.
Boy: Were you a man?
Girl: Yes, I was.
Boy: Were you American?
Girl: No, I wasn't.
Boy: Were you European?
Girl: Yes, I was.
Boy: So, dead, man and European. Did you live more than a hundred years ago?
Girl: Yes, I did.
Boy: Were you Italian?
Girl: Yes, I was.
Boy: Did you write books?

Girl:	No, I didn't.
Boy:	Were you a politician?
Girl:	No, I wasn't.
Boy:	Did you invent something?
Girl:	Yes, I did.
Boy:	Were you a famous inventor?
Girl:	Not really.
Boy:	So, you were famous for something else?
Girl:	Yes, I was.
Boy:	Um, more than a hundred years ago. An inventor. Were you Galileo?
Girl:	No, I wasn't.
Boy:	Were you a painter?
Girl:	Yes, I was.
Boy:	Were you …?

Answer
The famous person is Leonardo da Vinci.

4.2 A trip to remember
SB pages 28–29

1 Tell students about an interesting place you went to last year – or make one up! Students should work in pairs and ask and answer the questions in the exercise. Tell them they can make it up if they want to.

Check that students are forming the questions correctly, i.e.
When did you go?
How did you travel?
What did you do?
Who did you go with?
How much did it cost?
What did you see?
How long did you stay?

Listening

2 **KET Listening Part 5**

In Part 5 of the Listening paper, students will hear a monologue and they will need to write down information such as numbers, places, names, etc. It is a good idea to practise spelling out words aloud for this part of the test.

Ask students to look at the photos and talk about them.

The second photo was taken in the Louvre museum in Paris and the bottom photo is of a bateau mouche (a special sightseeing boat which cruises along the River Seine in Paris) with Notre Dame cathedral in the background.

Then play the recording and ask students to circle the correct answer.

Answers
1 5   2 5.30   3 £240   4 BERRI   5 boat trip

Recording script

About two years ago I went with my class on our first school trip – <u>five days</u> in Paris! There were about thirty of us and four teachers. We all went in one big coach from our school in London. The teachers told us to be at school at four thirty in the morning. Everyone was there on time, but the coach didn't arrive until five o'clock and <u>we didn't leave until five thirty</u>! We were very cold and tired.

Anyway, the coach was very comfortable and we watched a video and listened to some CDs on the journey. We had some sandwiches and drinks with us so we went straight to Paris without stopping. The trip was quite expensive. <u>It cost £240</u> and we wanted to save money so we didn't stop at motorway cafés. It only took us eight hours to reach Paris.

The name of the hotel in Paris was <u>the Hotel Berri – that's B-E-double R-I</u>. It was very old, but our room was nice and the bed was great – really soft! I shared the room with three other girls.

When we went shopping I tried to practise my French a few times but sometimes I didn't know the right words and spoke in English instead! The shops were great – I bought lots of presents, even a T-shirt for my little sister!

I think <u>what I most enjoyed was the river trip</u>. I took lots of photos of my friends and also of Notre Dame cathedral, and the wonderful art galleries.

I was sad to leave Paris. I had a lovely time there. We came home by coach and this time the journey was much shorter – we even arrived back half an hour early!

3 Ask students to read through the questions. Play the recording again, and ask the class to write down the answers. They may need to hear the recording once more. They should check their answers in pairs.

Answers
2 Yes, she did.
3 No, they didn't.
4 Yes, it did.
5 No, they didn't.
6 No, she didn't.
7 Yes, she did.
8 Yes, she did.
9 Yes, she did.
10 No, they didn't.

Ask students to work in pairs. They should underline the answers for exercise 3.

Now ask the class to underline all the descriptive adjectives in the recording script. They should then use a dictionary to find the opposite of each adjective.

Answers
first – last
big – small/little
cold – hot
tired – energetic
comfortable – uncomfortable
expensive – cheap
old – new
nice – horrible
great – awful
soft – hard
right – wrong
little – big
wonderful – terrible
sad – happy
lovely – horrible
shorter – longer

Ⓖrammar extra

4 Go through the examples of the use of *ago* in the box. Explain that we use *ago* to talk about a certain time period in the past. Explain that the other expressions in the box below – *yesterday, at breakfast*, etc. – are more precise times.

Go round the class asking questions so they understand the difference between a period of time and an exact time. Flashcards would be useful for this: one with *ago*, one with *at the weekend*, etc., so it could be held up and the student has to answer with that time expression.

Ask students to do the exercise in pairs.

Possible questions and answers
1 When did you last eat some chocolate?
   I ate some chocolate three hours ago.
2 When did you last email a friend?
   I emailed a friend two days ago.
3 When did you last read a magazine?
   I read a magazine last night.
4 When did you last listen to a CD?
   I listened to a CD twelve hours ago.
5 When did you last go to the cinema?
   I went to the cinema two weeks ago.
6 When did you last play football?
   I played football yesterday. / I don't play football.

7 When did you last do some homework?
   I did some homework at breakfast time.
8 When did you last go to an art gallery?
   I went to an art gallery last weekend.
9 When did you last buy some clothes?
   I bought some clothes on Saturday.
10 When did you last eat pizza?
   I ate pizza at lunch time.

5

Answers
1 Yesterday I *went* to the disco.
2 Who *did you go* to an art gallery with?
3 Last night I *had* a good dinner and saw a film.
4 Last year I went to New York and it *was* very interesting.
5 I *played* football with my brother on Saturday.
6 Tomas came to England two years ago.
7 Why *didn't you come* to see me?
8 (correct)
9 How much *did the trip cost*?
10 Shakespeare *wrote* many plays.

Activity

Answers
liked   saw
went   stayed
had   ate
took   began
arrived   travelled

l	l	q	u	b	s	d	e	t	s
i	d	w	t	a	t	a	t	e	t
k	d	w	a	t	k	r	r	u	a
e	s	e	r	o	j	r	j	k	y
d	a	n	g	o	k	i	s	w	e
m	b	t	f	k	t	v	a	d	d
p	u	i	h	f	c	e	w	i	c
b	e	g	a	n	s	d	r	v	x
o	z	a	d	p	d	a	t	u	i
l	t	r	a	v	e	l	l	e	d

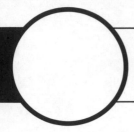

Units 1–4 Revision

SB pages 30–31

Speaking

1 Discuss the first sentence and the example answers with the whole class, then let them work through the others in pairs. If appropriate, have a brief whole class discussion of some of the other sentences and revise any language problems which have arisen as they talked in pairs.

Exercises 2–8 could be set for homework and discussed afterwards in class.

Vocabulary

2 Other answers may be correct depending on how they are justified.

3

Suggested answers
1 green – not a feeling
2 short – not a character adjective
3 friend – noun not adjective
4 house – you can't buy things there
5 coffee – you drink it not eat it
6 onion – only vegetable
7 hall – you don't eat there
8 bookshop – you buy things there

Writing

Answers			
1 vegetable	4 milk	7 fish	10 chocolate
2 snack	5 juice	8 carrot	11 potato
3 meat	6 grape	9 butter	12 chicken

4

Answers		
1 market	3 chemist	5 post office
2 newsagent	4 supermarket	

Grammar

5

Answers			
2 much	5 Does	8 Sometimes	11 Did
3 is	6 tell	9 doesn't	12 return
4 any	7 the	10 go	

6

Answers		
1 knew	5 taught	8 left
2 forgot	6 told	9 grew
3 said	7 wore	10 thought
4 sold		

7

Answers		
2 am/'m	9 'm/am	15 took
3 telephoned	10 like	16 saw
4 were	11 Are	17 were
5 needed	12 are / 're	18 Were
6 went	13 thought	19 look
7 Did you get	14 were	20 got
8 do you think		

8

Answers			
1 starts	4 their	7 at	9 wear
2 each	5 eat	8 Many	10 is
3 make	6 some		

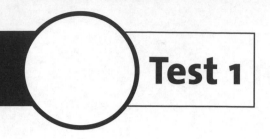

Test 1

Reading Part 1

Questions 1–5

Which notice (**A–H**) says this (**1–5**)?

For questions **1–5**, mark the correct letter **A–H**.

Example:

0 You can eat here in the evenings.   *Answer:* 0 A B C D E F G H

---

1 Children can do art lessons here.

2 Ask here about tours in the area.

3 Pay less for your holiday if you book it before April.

4 It is not possible to take any pictures here.

5 We have some cheap shoes for people with larger feet.

A
Hotel reception
We have information about day trips

B
No photographs please inside the museum

C
School holiday classes in painting and drawing (Tues and Thurs)

D
Jo's Restaurant
Open for dinner only

E
Camera for sale – ask inside

F
Photograph your children and win clothes, holidays or meals

G
Save money – £50 on all travel
(ends 31 March)

H
Half-price trainers
size 44 and above only

Writing Part 6

Questions 1–5

Read the descriptions of things you can buy in a department store.

What is the word for each one?

The first letter is already there. There is one space for each other letter in the word.

Example:

0 Buy this for a young child to play with.　　　　　　t _ _

　　　　　　　　　　　　　　　　　　　　　　　　　　Answer: | **0** | *toy* |

---

1 You use some of this when you wash your hair.　　s _ _ _ _ _ _

2 Wear these if the sun is hurting your eyes.　　　s _ _ _ _ _ _ _ _

3 You have this over your head when it is raining.　u _ _ _ _ _ _ _

4 Put this on your brush when you clean your teeth.　t _ _ _ _ _ _ _ _ _

5 You can buy this to wear over a T-shirt when it's cold.　s _ _ _ _ _ _

Listening Part 1

Questions 1–5

You will hear five short conversations.
You will hear each conversation twice.
There is one question for each conversation.
For questions **1–5**, put a tick (✓) under the right answer.

1 Where is Nick going to meet Karen?

A ☐

B ☐

C ☐

2 Where did the man go on holiday?

Turkey	**China**	**Italy**

A ☐   **B** ☐   **C** ☐

3 What time does the bookshop shut tonight?

A ☐

B ☐

C ☐

4 Which drink is Anna's?

A ☐

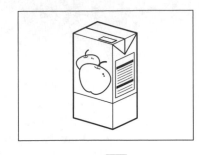

B ☐

C ☐

5 How much did David pay for his new camera?

A ☐

B ☐

C ☐

© Cambridge University Press, 2005

Test 1 Key

Reading Part 1

Answers

1 C   2 A   3 G   4 B   5 H

Writing Part 6

Answers

1 shampoo   3 umbrella   5 sweater
2 sunglasses   4 toothpaste

Listening Part 1

Answers

1 B   2 B   3 C   4 A   5 A

Recording script

Listening Part 1

You will hear five short conversations. You will hear each conversation twice. There is one question for each conversation. For questions 1 to 5 put a tick under the right answer.

1   Where is Nick going to meet Karen?

Nick: Karen, let's meet at the café after school. Then I can give you back your DVDs.

Karen: Sorry, Nick, I can't. I'm going swimming with Jenny. Why don't you come too? I'm meeting her at the bus stop at five o'clock.

Nick: OK. I'll go home and get my things and <u>see you at the pool</u> later.

Karen: Great.

Now listen again.

(The recording is repeated.)

2   Where did the man go on holiday?

Woman: Ian, tell me about your holiday. You went to Italy last week, didn't you?

Ian: Yes, but that was a business trip. <u>My holiday was three weeks in China</u> and it was really great.

Woman: How interesting. Can you bring in some photos tomorrow?

Ian: Fine, and you must show me your holiday photos of Turkey. I'd like to go there next.

Now listen again.

(The recording is repeated.)

3   What time does the bookshop shut tonight?

(On phone)

Woman: Blacks Books.

Man: Hello. Do you shut at six thirty tonight or is it later on Wednesdays?

Woman: It is, and <u>we're open until nine tonight</u> because there's a special talk at eight by John Franklin, the travel writer.

Man: Oh, I really want to see him. I'll be there at quarter to eight, then. Thanks.

Now listen again.

(The recording is repeated.)

4   Which drink is Anna's?

Boy: Can I sit down next to you, Anna? Here, you can have one of these cans of orange if you like.

Anna: No thanks, <u>I've got a bottle of water</u>. I want to go over and buy an apple. Do you know how much they are?

Boy: About 40p, I think. I'll keep your place at the table then.

Anna: Thanks.

Now listen again.

(The recording is repeated.)

5   How much did David pay for his new camera?

Woman: Hi, David. I like your new camera. I'm sure I saw that one in a shop for £85!

David: Oh, I didn't pay that much. <u>It only cost me £65</u> on the internet.

Woman: That's good. So have you still got some money left from your birthday?

David: Well, no. I had £75 but I bought a CD too.

Now listen again.

(The recording is repeated.)

5 Animals

5.1 A trip to the zoo	
Vocabulary	Animals; collocations with *do, make, take* and *spend*
Pronunciation	List intonation
Grammar extra	Lists with *and*
Exam skills	Listening Part 3: Multiple choice

5.2 An amazing animal	
Exam skills	Reading Part 5: Cloze
Grammar	Conjunctions: *and, but, because, or*
Spelling	*their, there, they're*

Preparation

Make copies of the *Collocation Snap* cards on page 120 and cut them up so that each student has ten cards.

5.1 A trip to the zoo

SB pages 32–33

Vocabulary

1 Ask the class to look at the pictures of animals and then do the exercise.

Answers

1 bear	5 elephant	8 spider
2 horse	6 dolphin	9 monkey
3 cat	7 fish	10 cow
4 dog		

2 This exercise can be done either in groups or as a class discussion.

Pronunciation

3 Play the recording of the examples in the Student's Book. Emphasise the falling intonation on the last word of a list.

Check that students are using the correct intonation as they are asking and answering amongst themselves and also when they are reporting back to the class.

Grammar extra

4 Refer students to the explanation in the Student's Book. Ask them to do the error correction exercise.

Answers
1 I saw a nice, colourful parrot at the zoo.
2 Yesterday we went to the zoo and the museum.
3 Susanna went out yesterday and took her dog for a walk.
4 There are many cats, dogs and horses at the farm.
5 The dolphins and (the) birds were near the boat.

Listening

5 The task here is designed to ease the students gently into a listening comprehension. Ask the class to look at the list of words. Play the recording and ask them to tick the words as they hear them. All the words are mentioned.

6 **KET Listening Part 3**

In Part 3 of the Listening paper candidates are given five multiple-choice questions on a dialogue that they hear. There is also an example.

Let students read through the questions carefully. Play the next track of the recording down as far as the example. After the example pause the recording and check that students understand what to do. Then play the rest of the recording.

Answers
1 A   2 C   3 B   4 A   5 B

Recording script

Listen to the example.
Mark: Natalie, what about going to the zoo at the weekend?
Natalie: Oh, sorry, Mark, but I'm going shopping on Saturday and I'm going to see my grandparents on Sunday, but I'm free in the week.
Mark: OK, then let's say Thursday.
Now listen to the rest of the conversation and answer the questions.
Natalie: Fine. It's cheaper then too. It's £8.00 for adults at the weekend. In the week we can get £1 off the normal student price of £7.50.

Mark: £6.50 – not bad! At the zoo, I've got to take some photographs of the animals for homework. My <u>art teacher</u> asked me and a friend to take as many as possible. It's lucky my mum bought me a camera for my birthday!

Natalie: Well, there are lots of different animals. They've got lions, bears and monkeys. I always love the monkeys – they make me laugh.

Mark: Let's visit them first then. <u>I need some photos of them.</u>

Natalie: OK, so how are we going to get there, Mark? Can your mum drive us there?

Mark: She'll be at work then. I think <u>the bus is best,</u> as the train is too expensive.

Natalie: Fine, but I need to be home by six thirty.

Mark: Well, that's no problem because <u>it shuts at five thirty.</u> We'll be tired anyway, so why don't we leave at half past four?

Natalie: That's great! See you soon, then.

Mark: Bye!

Vocabulary

7 Explain that some words in English go together. We call these collocations. Refer to the example, which is taken from the recording.

Ask the class to work through the exercise in pairs. Some nouns can be used more than once. Sometimes there is a non-literal meaning – for example *to make money*. This means to earn money from a job.

> **Answers**
> to do – homework, the shopping, nothing
> to make – a phone call, an appointment, a cake, some
> money, breakfast, time
> to take – photographs, a phone call, an exam
> to spend – time, some money

E xtension activity

Collocation Snap
Photocopy and cut up the Collocation Snap cards on page 120 and give each student ten cards.

Students play in pairs. They put their cards in a pile, face down. They take it in turns to turn over their top card. If it collocates with the card their partner has just turned over, they get a point if they can say a sentence using the collocation.

8 This exercise can be done in class or for homework.

> **Answers**
> | 2 did | 4 make | 6 made |
> |---|---|---|
> | 3 did | 5 took | |

9 Students form pairs and discuss the questions using the collocations they have learnt.

> **Vocabulary extension:** collocations with *have*:
> *have a shower, breakfast, a party, a drink, a walk, a cold, an appointment, some money, time*

5.2 An amazing animal
SB pages 34–35

1 Tell students to cover the text on polar bears at the bottom of the page and work through the quiz in pairs, discussing whether the answers are a) or b).

Reading

2

> **Answers** to the quiz in exercise 1
> | 1 a | 4 a | 7 b |
> |---|---|---|
> | 2 b | 5 a | 8 b |
> | 3 a | 6 b | 9 a |

Check for understanding and any unknown vocabulary.

Grammar

3 Refer students to the underlined examples in the text. There is an additional exercise in the Grammar folder on page 138 of the Student's Book that they can do for homework or in class.

> **Answers**
> We use *because, and, but* and *or* to join two clauses to make one longer sentence.
>
> 1 because 2 or 3 and 4 but

4 **KET Reading Part 5**

In Reading Part 5, students read through a text and identify the appropriate structural word (auxiliary, modal, determiner, pronoun, preposition, conjunction, etc.) that is gapped. There are eight three-option multiple-choice questions plus an integrated example.

5 Students decide which conjunction to use to join each sentence together: *and*, *or*, *but* or *because*. In some of these examples a case can be made for one or more of the alternatives.

E xtension activity

Ask the class to work in groups. Each group chooses an animal. They must write down sentences about their animal. For example:

I have a dog. I take her for walks because she needs exercise. I feed her meat and give her water to drink. She also likes chocolate chips or biscuits to eat. She likes playing with me, but not with my cat.

When students have finished, they should read out their sentences to the class. They get a point for each correct sentence.

S pelling spot

6 These words are often confused by students at this level. Go through the examples and ask the class to do the exercise.

7

Activity

This exercise recycles vocabulary and intonation. Remind students to use the listing intonation they practised earlier in the unit. Start off the game by saying: *I went to the zoo and I saw a lion.*

Exam folder 3

Reading Part 2   Multiple choice

SB page 36

Ask students to read the information about this part of the Reading and Writing paper. Elicit more words to go under the headings: verbs, nouns, adjectives, adverbs, collocations. Put them on the board.

Give students time to read through the Exam advice and check for understanding. Draw their attention to the sample answer sheet and make sure they know how to fill it in correctly.

Ask the students to do the Part 2 task. Explain that there is only one correct answer. Use the example question (**0**) to show why **B** is the answer. This is because the verb *enjoy* is followed by an *-ing* form.

Rebecca and Tom <u>want to visit</u> their uncle's farm.

Rebecca and Tom <u>agree to visit</u> their uncle's farm.

Ask the students to write sentences showing how the other words are used.

Reading Part 5   Multiple-choice cloze

SB page 37

For this part of the exam students read a text with eight three-option multiple-choice questions. There is also an example.

Ask the students to look at the types of word which are tested. They should match parts of speech 1–7 with examples a–g.

Answers			
1 c	3 e	5 g	7 b
2 d	4 f	6 a	

Ask the students to do the Part 5 task. When they have finished they should compare answers with a partner and justify their decisions. Again, students might find it useful to write a sentence showing how the wrong options are used.

Answers		
28 C	31 A	34 C
29 A	32 B	35 A
30 B	33 A	

6 Leisure and hobbies

6.1 Theme park fun	
Reading	Reading for information
Exam skills	Speaking Part 2: Activity
Grammar	Comparative and superlative adjectives
Spelling	Comparative and superlative adjectives

6.2 Free time	
Exam skills	Listening Part 4: Note taking
Grammar extra	Comparative adverbs
Exam skills	Reading Part 3: On the telephone
	Writing Part 9: Common spelling mistakes
Pronunciation	/ə/ as in short*er*, moth*er*

6.1   Theme park fun

SB pages 38–39

1   Invite the class to look at the photos of the rides at different theme parks. Ask them to discuss, in pairs, which one they prefer and then go on to talk about theme parks in general.

B ackground information

The photos are of:
(left) *Roar* at Six Flags park in the USA. It is wooden and was built in 1998.
(centre) a rollercoaster in California
(right) *Colossus* at Thorpe Park in the UK. It is made of steel and was built in 2002.
(bottom) *Dodonpa* at Fujikuyu Highland park in Japan

2   Ask students to look at the two leaflets about the theme parks. They should consider all the information and discuss in pairs which one they would like to go to. Open this up to a class discussion – this activity should only take 5–10 minutes at most.

3   **KET Speaking Part 2**

The usual format for the Speaking test is two candidates and two examiners. One examiner, the interlocutor, will ask the questions and the other examiner, the assessor,

will write down the marks. Part 2 lasts about 3–4 minutes and during that time the candidates will talk to each other. They will be given cards with prompt material containing factual information of a non-personal kind.

This exercise is initial practice for Part 2 of the Speaking test. In the test itself, the candidates cannot see each other's cards.

Ask students to form pairs and decide who is Student A and who is Student B.

Student A should ask Student B questions about Fantasma.

Student B should ask Student A questions about Alien Adventure.

They should answer using the information in the leaflets.

> **Possible questions**
> 1 How many rides does Fantasma / Alien Adventure have?
> 2 Which dates is Fantasma / Alien Adventure open?
> 3 What are the opening hours for Fantasma / Alien Adventure?
> 4 How many visitors does Fantasma / Alien Adventure have a year?
> 5 How many hotel rooms does Fantasma / Alien Adventure have?
> 6 How much does a family ticket cost at Fantasma / Alien Adventure?

4   Students should work through this exercise, which is the introduction to comparative adjectives.

> **Answers**
> 1 newer
> 2 shorter
> 3 smaller
> 4 more
> 5 more
> 6 better

Grammar

5   Students should find examples in exercise 4 to fill in the gaps in this exercise. This will provide them with the basic rules of how to form a comparative adjective.

Reading

6 Ask students if they know which theme parks are the biggest and best in the world. They should then read the text to see if their park is mentioned.

Grammar

7 The words underlined in the text in exercise 6 are superlative adjectives. Ask students to use the information given to complete exercise 7 with superlative adjectives. Refer them to the Grammar folder on page 138 of the Student's Book for an additional exercise. This can be done in class or for homework.

E xtension activity

Ask students to make as many words in English as they can out of the letters in the word 'rollercoaster'. They can use an English–English dictionary to help them. The student with the most words, and who can explain what they all mean, wins.

S pelling spot

8 Check students understand the rules and ask them to complete the chart.

E xtension activity

Ask the class to form groups of four to six.
Everyone in the group has to form a line according to the instructions they are given. For example: *Form a line according to how long your hair is. The person with the shortest hair goes at the front.*

The winners are the team who form a line correctly in the shortest time. Each person in the team must be able to say a correct sentence in English using a comparative or superlative adjective, e.g. *My hair is longer than Sarah's. Jeans's got the shortest hair*, etc. If they can't do this, their team is disqualified.

Students can do this activity to talk about:
size of feet
size of pet / number of pets
number of brothers and sisters in family
height

6.2 Free time

SB pages 40–41

1 Students should work in pairs to discuss the questions. Then they should look at the pictures and ask and answer questions about other things they do in their free time.

Listening

2 **KET Listening Part 4**

KET Listening Part 4 is similar to Part 5, in that both are note-taking exercises. However, Part 4 is a conversation whereas Part 5 is a monologue.

Ask students to predict the sort of word the answers will be in this exercise. For example: Is the answer to 1 a number or a word? Is it a price or a time? What do you think the missing word is in 4? What do cafés sell?

This may seem very easy to do, but it is worth pointing out to students that it would be very helpful for them to do this in the exam, as it will give them some idea of what they are listening for.

Recording script

Man: Hello, Aqua Park. Can I help you?
Girl: Yes, please. I'd like some information. Are you open on Saturdays?
Man: We're open every day. From nine in the morning until six, but on Saturdays we close much later, <u>at ten</u>.
Girl: OK. And how much does it cost?
Man: Adults are £15 and children £10, but families can get in more cheaply with a family ticket – <u>only £50</u>.
Girl: And do you have a large car park? I'm coming from London.
Man: We have four car parks. From London it's much easier for you to park in the one in Glendennan Road.

Girl: I'll write that down. Can you spell the name of the road for me?

Man: It's G-L-E-N-D-E-double N-A-N.

Girl: And is there anywhere to get food and drink?

Man: Yes, there's a restaurant for hot food. There's also a café for <u>ice cream</u> and drinks.

Girl: Is there anything else I need to know? Do you have a shop?

Man: Yes. It sells sweets, newspapers, and you can get <u>books</u> there, too.

Girl: That's great. Thank you.

E xtension activity

Students need lots of practice at listening to words being spelt out. The letters G/J, B/V/P, N/M, A/E/I, W/U/Y are particularly hard to hear. They also need to practise numbers, especially 14/40, 15/50, etc.

Ask students to choose a place that they go to in their free time – a swimming pool, shop, cinema, etc. They should write down as much information about the place as they can, e.g. opening times, address, what type of place it is, etc. Students can change the information slightly if the places are too well known.

Now ask them to write down a list of questions they might want to ask, e.g.
- *Where is it?*
- *What does it sell?*
- *When does it open/close?*

Students then form pairs and ask and answer questions about their place. If Student A doesn't know the answer to a question he or she can say 'I don't know'. Student B is allowed to ask Student A to repeat the answer or to spell the word aloud.

G rammar extra

If students aren't sure what the difference is between an adjective and an adverb, remind them that adjectives give extra information about nouns, whereas adverbs give extra information about verbs. For example:

The car goes *fast* (adverb). It's a *fast* (adjective) car. It goes *faster* (comparative adverb) than yours. It's a *faster* (comparative adjective) car than yours.

I worked *hard* (adverb) today. I'm a *hard* (adjective) worker. I worked *harder* (comparative adverb) than you did. I'm the *hardest* (superlative adjective) worker in the class.

3 Students should complete the exercise either in class or at home.

Answers

1 sooner	4 earlier	7 nearer
2 harder	5 longer	8 more carefully
3 more quietly	6 better	

4 **KET Reading Part 3**

Reading Part 3 deals with functional English.

Put the following on the board:
Julia Jones
9256784
Hello, Julia speaking.

Ask students when they would say these phrases. Elicit – when answering the telephone.

Ask students to work in pairs to put each conversation in order. The first conversation is less formal than the second. Play the recording to check their answers when they are ready. Notice that when referring to themselves English people say: ***It's Lisa***, ***It's Mrs Jones***, etc.

Answers
Conversation 1
The order is:
1 h **2** f **3** d **4** b **5** c **6** g **7** a **8** e

Conversation 2
The order is:
1 j **2** b **3** g **4** c **5** d **6** h **7** f **8** i **9** e **10** a

Recording script

Conversation 1
Lisa: Hello?
Paula: Hi, is that Serena?
Lisa: No, it's Lisa.
Paula: Oh, hi, Lisa. It's Paula here. Is Serena in?
Lisa: No, she's out shopping. Can I take a message?
Paula: Just tell her I rang about going swimming tomorrow.
Lisa: OK. No problem. Bye.
Paula: Bye.

Conversation 2
Man: Hello. Can I help you?
Woman: Good morning. I'd like to book tickets for the film tonight, please.
Man: That's fine. How many would you like?
Woman: Three – that's for two adults and one child.
Man: And your name?
Woman: It's Wilkinson, W-I-L-K-I-N-S-O-N.
Man: Can you collect them by 7 o'clock?
Woman: Yes, no problem. Thank you.
Man: Thanks very much. Bye.
Woman: Bye.

5 KET Writing Part 9

These mistakes are taken from KET scripts and are the most common ones that are made at this level. Although a few spelling errors are acceptable at KET, it is better to keep these to a minimum. It may be a good idea to make a poster and put up words which the class has trouble spelling, so that they are there as a constant reminder.

Answers
friend
beautiful
because
interesting
there
which

Pronunciation

6 The focus is on the unstressed vowel sound /ə/, as at the end of *camera*. Draw students' attention to the picture. Then ask them to listen and repeat.

7 Check that students understand how a crossword puzzle works and that *Across* and *Down* are clear instructions. This could be done at home or in class. Check that students pronounce the answers clearly.

Answers

Across	*Down*
5 interesting	**1** computer
6 cinema	**2** longer
8 father	**3** letter
9 America	**4** listen
	6 camera
	7 alone

Activity

Divide the class into two groups, A and B. Group A is going to ask questions about free time activities at home. Group B is going to ask questions about free time physical activities. Students should use the questionnaires on page 128 of their Student's Books.

Give students some time to read their questionnaire and write a few more questions.

Students should then go round the class asking the questions to students from the other group. In order to find out how many people do the activity, they will need to put a tick to represent each person next to the question.

When they have completed their questionnaires ask them to report back to the class, using comparative and superlatives where possible, for example:
Most people watch TV every night.
The largest number of people go swimming.
People think chess is the least interesting game.
More people like playing computer games than watching TV.

Exam folder 4

Listening Parts 4 and 5
Note taking

SB pages 42–43

Ask students to read the information about Parts 4 and 5 of the Listening paper.

Ask the students to work in pairs. Student A should give Student B the information and spell out any words that are necessary. Student B should write the information down.

Remind students that when saying telephone numbers 0 is pronounced *oh* and 33 is pronounced *double three*. With dates we write *1st August* and we say *the first of August*.

Refer the class to the Exam advice box and check they understand the information.

Part 4

Students should have a quick look through the questions to get an idea of what they are listening for. There is no extra time given for this in the exam. Part 4 is a conversation between two people.

Recording script

Questions 16 to 20. You will hear a woman asking about a guitar for sale. Listen and complete questions 16 to 20. You will hear the coversation twice.

Man: 669872.
Woman: Oh, hello. I'm ringing about the guitar you have for sale. Can you tell me what make it is?
Man: It's a <u>Fender</u>.
Woman: And how old is it?
Man: Well, I bought it from a friend about six months ago, and he was given it for his birthday, so it's about <u>eleven</u> months old now.
Woman: How much are you selling it for?
Man: Umm, I think I'd like <u>two hundred</u> pounds for it. I bought it for four hundred.
Woman: Sounds good. Can I come and see it?
Man: Sure. I live at 60, Kensal Road. That's <u>K-E-N-S-A-L</u> Road.
Woman: Can I walk there from the High Street?
Man: It's probably best if you get a bus. The number <u>eighteen</u> bus stops in my road outside number seventy.
Woman: I'm free tonight. Would about eight o'clock be OK?
Man: A bit later? After <u>nine thirty</u> is better for me as I don't get back from work until eight.
Woman: My name is Jenny Levine and you are …?
Man: Josh Bentley.
Woman: See you tonight then.

Now listen again.
(The recording is repeated.)

Part 5

Ask students to look at Part 5. They should try to predict the answers. Part 5 is a monologue.

Recording script

Questions 21 to 25. You will hear some information about an activity centre. Listen and complete questions 21 to 25. You will hear the information twice.

Woman: Thank you for calling High Cross Activity Centre. The Centre is open from <u>March to October</u> and we have things to do for all ages. At High Cross you can play football or try our new climbing wall, and you can also learn to play <u>tennis</u>. It costs £15 to come for a day and for this you get your classes and lunch in our restaurant. One week's stay is <u>£325</u> for a room and all meals. It is cheaper if you come here as part of a group. We are happy to accept group bookings, especially from companies and schools. Group sizes can be from five to <u>eighteen</u> people. If you would like to talk about what we do here, then ring our Manager, Pete Wright, that's <u>W-R-I-G-H-T</u>. Office hours are nine o'clock until five thirty and the number to ring is <u>8775980</u>. After five thirty you can ring Pete's mobile on 0770 5566328.

Now listen again.
(The recording is repeated.)

7 Clothes

7.1 The latest fashion

Exam skills	Reading Part 4: Right, Wrong, Doesn't say
Grammar	Simple and continuous tenses
Spelling	*-ing* form

7.2 Your clothes

Vocabulary	Clothes; adjectives to describe clothes
Listening	Listening for specific information
Pronunciation	The last letters of the alphabet: *w, x, y, z*
Exam skills	Reading Part 3: Short conversations

Preparation

You will need a hat and dice for each team of six students for the Activity in 7.2.

7.1 The latest fashion
SB pages 44–45

1 Ask students to do this warm-up activity in small groups, encouraging them to use the sentence openers given. Elicit information about favourite T-shirts.

Reading

2 **KET Reading Part 4**

Explain that in a Reading Part 4 task of this type it is a good idea to look through the sentences before reading the text, to see what is being tested. Suggest students discuss whether the sentences are right or wrong in pairs. Don't spend much time eliciting answers at this stage.

3 Before students read the text, point out the third possibility (*Doesn't say*). Explain that students should only choose this option if there is no information to confirm or reject the sentence in the text. They should *not* base the answer on their own knowledge, but only on what is in the text.

Answers
1 Right
2 Right
3 Wrong – It was later than this.
4 Wrong – This happened in the mid-1960s.
5 Doesn't say
6 Doesn't say
7 Wrong – It cost 'well over' £100.

B ackground information

- Marlon Brando died in 2004, aged 80. He has starred in many films, including *The Godfather* and *Apocalypse Now*.
- James Dean died young in a car crash.
- Jean Seberg made more than 30 films until her death in Paris in 1979.
- Thanks to the 'Free Angela' campaign, Angela Davis was eventually released from prison in 1972. She is now a professor and gives lectures all over the world on issues of social justice.

Grammar

4 Ask students to read the example sentences in the timeline and fill in the missing dates. Note that two different tenses are used in the sentences (the past simple and past continuous) but don't point this out to students until exercise 5.

Answers
1 1954
2 1955
3 1959
4 1960

5 Ask students to identify the tense of each underlined verb and elicit reasons for why the two different tenses are used in sentence 3. Refer them to the notes in the Grammar folder on page 139 if necessary.

Answers
1 the present continuous (temporary)
2 the present simple (habitual)
3 the past continuous (*was wearing* = temporary in the past) and past simple (*fell* = completed action)

6 This exercise focuses on forming the past continuous. Make sure students give you both affirmative and negative sentences.

7 Ask students to fill in the missing verbs in the timeline in pairs and then complete the story.

Answers
Timeline
10.20 – 10.45   was looking at
10.35   saw
10.45   started
10.46   left

Story
2 saw
3 was trying on
4 decided
5 said
6 went
7 found
8 was waiting
9 started
10 left

8 This exercise provides further practice in past tenses. If time is short, the sentences can be set for homework.

Answers
2 bought
3 was wearing; looked
4 was wearing; stopped; changed
5 was waiting; drove; gave
6 was living; heard

S pelling spot

Explain that the *-ing* form of many verbs requires a spelling change. Ask students to look at the examples carefully.

9 Ask students to write the *-ing* forms on their own. Students can then take turns to write their answers on the board.

Answers
break	breaking
leave	leaving
make	making
throw	throwing
stay	staying
lend	lending
sit	sitting
win	winning

7.2   Your clothes
SB pages 46–47

1 Give students two or three minutes to discuss their favourite clothes and explain where they buy them.

Vocabulary

2 Elicit answers round the class.

Answers
1 boots
2 two hats
3 two belts
4 sweater
5 tights
6 suit
7 two baseball caps
8 jacket
9 jeans
10 shirt
11 trainers
12 skirt
13 shoes
14 shorts
15 socks
16 trousers
17 coat

3

Answers
A couple of means two of something, not necessarily identical things; *a pair of* describes things that are used together (e.g. *socks, shoes*), sometimes referring to plural nouns (e.g. *scissors, trousers*).

Pictures 1, 5, 9, 11, 13, 14, 15 and 16 show pairs of things.

4 Check understanding of the nouns listed, for example *pocket, button, zip*. Ask students to use some of the adjectives and nouns in their descriptions.

E xtension activity

Suggest students prepare a class exhibition on clothes and fashion, using vocabulary they have learned in this unit. They can bring in photographs from magazines or research internet websites for information. Organise them into groups and suggest different topics they could prepare – for example, the clothes of a famous designer, today's top fashion models, what clothes are made of, the history of shoes. They should write short texts to go with any pictures, for display on the classroom wall.

Listening

5 This listening task practises the general skill of listening for specific information. Play the recording twice if necessary. Ask students to put ticks in the table as they listen and then compare answers in pairs.

Answers
Speaker 1, Ben:	shorts and (two) T-shirts
Speaker 2, Louisa:	jacket
Speaker 3, Chris:	trousers and cap

Recording script

Speaker 1: I work as a waiter on Wednesday evenings and I save most of the money I earn. My dad said I should buy some new trousers for work, but yesterday I saw this pair of <u>yellow cotton shorts</u>, with lots of pockets and zips. They looked wonderful, and <u>I decided to get them</u> for the summer, with a couple of extra <u>T-shirts</u>. Dad still thinks I need some trousers, but my boss doesn't mind what I wear!

Speaker 2: There was this beautiful Italian leather <u>jacket</u> in the sale. It was soft black leather, with a pocket on each side. I tried it on over a red shirt I was wearing at the time, and it looked so cool. But the thing was that it cost well over £200, even in the sale! In the end, my mum lent me half the money. <u>I'm really pleased I got it</u>. It'll stay in fashion for years, I'm sure.

Speaker 3: I don't buy many clothes. Until last Saturday, I had two pairs of jeans and some T-shirts and that was about it. But I saw a great pair of baggy <u>trousers</u> in town, dark green and really well cut. My girlfriend was with me when I tried them on. She hated them. She prefers me in jeans, you see. Anyway, <u>I decided to get them</u>. <u>I bought this cap</u> in the same colour, too. Nice, isn't it?

Pronunciation

6 The last letters of the alphabet can get forgotten! Play the recording of Speaker 1, Ben, which contains various examples of *w*, *x*, *y* and *z*. Ask students to complete the sentences and repeat what they hear. Draw students' attention to the pictures, which will help them to remember the sounds /w/ as in *waiter*, /ks/ as in *taxi*, /j/ as in *yellow* and /z/ as in *zebra*.

Answers
1 work; waiter; Wednesday
2 yesterday; yellow
3 zips
4 wonderful
5 extra

7

Recording script and answers

1 zoo
2 wool
3 young
4 excellent
5 zero
6 water
7 year
8 expensive

Reading

8 **KET Reading Part 3**

In this first part of Reading Part 3, students are given two-line conversations covering situations in everyday English. Suggest students try out all three options in each conversation before choosing their answers.

Answers
1 B   2 C   3 A   4 C   5 B

Activity

Explain that the activity practises the spelling of clothes vocabulary. Students in each group should take it in turns to choose the words to be spelled and check correct spelling with you or in a dictionary if necessary.

Writing folder 2

Writing Part 7   Open cloze

SB pages 48–49

Ask students to read the information about this part of the Reading and Writing paper.

1 Ask students to add more words to each set and compare examples in pairs.

Possible answers
articles:	an, the
pronouns:	me, its
prepositions:	on, in
quantifiers:	any, every
auxiliary verbs:	has, had
modal verbs:	must, should

2 Elicit answers quickly.

Answers
1 you (pronoun)
2 did/do (auxiliary)
3 to (preposition)
4 should (modal)
5 any (quantifier)
6 a (article)

3 Remind students that in the exam there may be two short texts, like these postcards. This type of guided task can be useful as exam preparation for weaker students. Using a Part 7 task from any KET past paper, give students two or three options for each space, including the correct answers. In this way, students will become more familiar with the task and gain enough confidence to tackle the 'open' spaces.

Answers

1 in	5 our	8 Did
2 some	6 from	9 because
3 until	7 much	10 the
4 must		

Part 7

Ask students to read the Exam advice and do the task on their own. Elicit answers. Alternatively, this exam task can be done as homework.

Answers

41 some	45 because/where	48 on
42 me	46 it	49 are
43 There	47 much	50 my
44 for		

8 Entertainment

8.1 A great movie	
Grammar	Modal verbs 1: *can, may, must*
Exam skills	Reading Part 5: Multiple-choice cloze

8.2 Cool sounds	
Vocabulary	Music and concerts
Exam skills	Listening Part 1: Short conversations
Pronunciation	Short questions
Spelling	Mistakes with vowels

8.1 A great movie

SB pages 50–51

1 Elicit the English titles of the films: the pictures show the films, (top left) *Lord of the Rings 3*, (top right) *The Matrix Reloaded* and (bottom) *Titanic*. Lead a brief class discussion on the popularity of these films, using the phrases given. If your students are not familiar with these films, ask them which of the features listed are most important in a film.

2 Students ask each other the questions about films.

Grammar

3

> **Answers**
> 1 I <u>can</u> understand most films in French.
> 2 Jenny <u>may</u> buy that DVD, but she's not sure.
> 3 You <u>must</u> book in advance for the new Tom Cruise film.
> 4 I <u>had to</u> take my passport to the cinema to show my age.
> 5 When he was in New York, Roberto <u>could</u> choose to see a different movie every night.

Note that *have to* is also commonly used in the present tense. Its usage is slightly different from *must* but, at KET level, students needn't worry about the distinction. Note also that *might* can be used instead of *may* for possibility (but is not tested at KET).

4 This provides students with an explanation and example of when we use each modal verb.

> **Answers**
> b 4   c 2   d 1   e 5

5 Ask students to complete the notes and examples in pairs. Elicit answers.

> **Completed notes**
> • We cannot use the word *must* in the past. Instead, we use *had to*.
>   Example: *Last night, I had to do my homework.*
> • When we are talking about something we are unable to do, we use the word *cannot* or the contracted form *can't*.
>   Example: *I can't ride a horse, but I'd like to be able to.*
> • If we are talking about something we were unable to do in the past, we use *could not* or the contracted form *couldn't*.
>   Example: *Before I was five, I couldn't read, but now I can.*

6 Ask students to complete the exercise on their own. Elicit answers round the class.

> **Answers**
> 2 had to   4 could   6 must   8 must
> 3 couldn't   5 Can   7 may

7 Ask students to complete the table and then work in groups of four or five. Encourage them to expand a little when comparing their answers, e.g. *I can't ski black runs and I never want to. I may drive a car one day.*

E xtension activity

Ask students to prepare a similar chart focusing on a past event, for example a visit to the cinema, using *had to, could, couldn't*. Verb phrases could include *book seats on the internet, queue for tickets, sit together, buy a drink*, etc. Elicit their suggestions and put an example table on the board.

Reading

8   KET Reading Part 5

The photo shows Carrie-Anne Moss as Trinity in *The Matrix*. This exam-level task can be set for homework if time is short.

> **Answers**
> 2 C   4 A   6 C   8 B
> 3 B   5 C   7 A

8.2 Cool sounds

SB pages 52–53

1 Ask students to discuss their top bands and then take a class vote on the most popular band.

Vocabulary

2 Suggest students work on the word square in pairs and then use the words to describe the photo. The band in the photo is *Moloko*.

> **Answers**
> play, dance, guitar, bass, speakers, singer, lights, drums, piano, concert
>
> | s | l | o | u | b | s | p | l | a | y |
> |---|---|---|---|---|---|---|---|---|---|
> | i | d | w | t | a | t | i | t | e | y |
> | n | d | w | a | t | d | a | n | c | e |
> | g | u | i | t | a | r | n | j | o | x |
> | e | l | n | g | o | u | o | w | n | e |
> | r | i | t | f | k | m | v | s | c | i |
> | p | g | b | a | s | s | a | u | e | c |
> | b | h | e | a | n | s | m | r | r | e |
> | o | t | a | m | r | d | a | t | t | i |
> | l | s | p | e | a | k | e | r | s | d |
>
> **Possible answers**
> The band has a singer. She may be dancing.
> Two men are playing the guitar.
> There are some big speakers.
> We can see some drums.
> There are lights. It looks like a concert.

Listening

3 **KET Listening Part 1**

These conversations are at KET level, but in the exam there would be a wider range of topics, rather than this single focus on music. Remind students that the questions are also recorded. You will hear each recording twice.

> **Answers**
> 1 A 2 B 3 C 4 B 5 A

Recording script

1 How much did Craig earn from the concert?

Boy: The band earned ninety pounds last night. That's the best yet!

Girl: But what did they pay you, Craig? You booked the concert, so you should earn more than the other two.

Boy: I don't agree. We took <u>thirty pounds</u> each and that's fine.

Girl: Well, they must give you half next time. Forty-five pounds sounds right to me!

Now listen again.

(The recording is repeated.)

2 Which band did the girl see?

Girl: I saw a good band at last Saturday's rock festival. The singer was great!

Boy: The band with the piano player? He sang well, didn't he?

Girl: I didn't see anything with a piano. This singer was called Queen Cat. She could really dance too.

Boy: Oh, I know who you mean – <u>the band had three guitars</u>. Yes, excellent.

Now listen again.

(The recording is repeated.)

3 Where is the next band from?

Boy: Who's on next, Kate? Is it that Brazilian band? They're great!

Girl: Yeah, they are, but they're not on until this evening. It's a new band from <u>Iceland</u> now … you know, where Bjork's from.

Boy: Sounds interesting. I enjoyed that last band from Australia. Did you?

Girl: No, they were boring.

Now listen again.

(The recording is repeated.)

4 What does Ben play?

Boy: Hi, Anna. Tell me, is your brother <u>Ben still playing the drums</u>? We want someone tonight because Ray's ill.

Girl: Is he? <u>Ben still plays</u>, but he's away this week. I'm learning the piano you know.

Boy: Great. Perhaps you can play in our band one day then!

Girl: Can I? Ben says the guitar's a better choice because all bands have guitar players.

Now listen again.

(The recording is repeated.)

5 What must Kim bring to the party?

Girl: Hello, Kim? Listen, I want some special lights for my party tonight. Can you bring some?

Boy: Sorry, Tracey, I can't. Try the music shop in town. Do you want to borrow my guitar tonight?

Girl: No thanks, but <u>don't forget your Eminem CDs</u>. I'll phone the shop about the lights now.

Boy: OK. See you later.

Now listen again.

(*The recording is repeated.*)

Pronunciation

4 Play the example of short questions. Explain that using short questions like Anna does is a good way of sounding more natural in English. Then pause the recording and make sure students understand what they have to do.

Remind students to listen carefully to the verb that is used in each sentence, so they know which auxiliary verb to use in the question. Refer them back to the example with Anna if necessary.

Play the recording, which has a short pause after each statement for students to write the sentence number next to the question.

Then let students listen to both parts of the conversations to check their answers.

> **Answers**
> **1** Did I?
> **2** Have you?
> **3** Aren't they?
> **4** Can't you?
> **5** Isn't it?
> **6** Did they?

Recording script

(NB The sentences are recorded twice: the first time you will hear sentences 1 to 6 with Speaker 1 only, with a pause for students to write their answers; the second time you will also hear Speaker 2, so that students can check their answers.)

1
Speaker 1: You left these CDs at the party.
(*pause*)
Speaker 2: Did I?

2
Speaker 1: I've got tickets for *Radiohead's* next concert.
(*pause*)
Speaker 2: Have you?

3
Speaker 1: Jon and Alice aren't coming to see the band now.
(*pause*)
Speaker 2: Aren't they?

4
Speaker 1: We went to Glastonbury last summer but we can't this year.
(*pause*)
Speaker 2: Can't you?

5
Speaker 1: The next band's not on until midnight.
(*pause*)
Speaker 2: Isn't it?

6
Speaker 1: *Coldplay* played six songs from their new CD.
(*pause*)
Speaker 2: Did they?

5 Play the recording, this time asking students to say the short question and add a short phrase after it. Pause the recording if they need extra time.

> **Possible answers**
> **1** Did I? Thanks.
> **2** Have you? Great news! / How wonderful!
> **3** Aren't they? What a pity. / Never mind.
> **4** Can't you? Never mind. / What a pity.
> **5** Isn't it? That's bad. / Never mind.
> **6** Did they? How wonderful!

6 The questions not used in exercise 4 are *Must I?*, *Don't you?* and *Couldn't she?* Ask students to write the conversations in pairs and then elicit answers.

S pelling spot

7 The spelling errors featured here are among the most common ones in the *Cambridge Learner Corpus* at KET level.

> **Answers**
> **1** Yesterday I was at a *beautiful* rock concert.
> **2** It's my *favourite* cinema.
> **3** I'm selling my piano *because* I don't want it any more.
> **4** A lot of *tourists* visit my town.
> **5** I went to a nightclub with my *friends*.
> **6** There are two *museums* in the town.

Activity

The photo is of Eminem. Suggest students work on similar pictures of famous people in disguise and bring them to the next lesson. They should include some sentences about the star as clues.

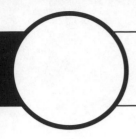

Units 5–8 Revision

SB pages 54–55

This revision unit recycles the language and topics from Units 5–8, as well as providing exam practice for Reading Part 5 and Writing Part 7.

Speaking

1 Encourage students to say as much as possible about each sentence.

Grammar

2

> **Answers**
> 1 C   2 B   3 C   4 A

3

> **Answers**
> 2 C   3 A   4 B   5 C   6 C   7 B   8 A

Vocabulary

4

> **Answers**
> 2 hot   4 boring   6 fast   8 small
> 3 closed   5 old   7 thin

5 Encourage students to record new vocabulary in topic groups.

> **Answers**
> *Animals:* bear, dolphin, elephant, fish, horse, monkey, snake
> *Clothes:* blouse, button, jacket, pocket, shorts, socks, trainers, zip
> *Music:* concert, drums, guitar, piano, song
> *Activities:* chess, climbing, cycling, skateboarding, table tennis

Writing

6

> **Answers**
> 1 to
> 2 It
> 3 were
> 4 more
> 5 at/in/inside
> 6 best/greatest/coolest
> 7 because/as
> 8 his
> 9 may/might/could
> 10 why

Test 2

Reading Part 2

Questions 1–5

Read the sentences about shopping for shoes.
Choose the best word (**A**, **B** or **C**) for each space.

For questions **1–5**, mark **A**, **B** or **C**.

Example:

0 Manuela .... some lovely shoes yesterday.

   A saw   **B** watched   **C** looked

Answer:

---

1 They were in the .... of a large shop.

   A shelf   **B** window   **C** table

2 She decided to .... them on.

   A take   **B** turn   **C** try

3 The lady in the shoe shop was very .... at helping Manuela.

   A excellent   **B** great   **C** good

4 Manuela .... over £100 on the shoes.

   A bought   **B** spent   **C** paid

5 She came home with a nice pair of .... too.

   A socks   **B** skirts   **C** belts

© Cambridge University Press, 2005

Reading Part 5

Read the article about clothes.
Choose the best word (**A**, **B** or **C**) for each space.

For questions **6–13**, mark **A**, **B** or **C**.

DIFFERENT CLOTHES

Years ago it (**0**) .... quite easy to tell what country a person was from by looking (**6**) .... his or her clothes. But today, with the internet and cheap travel, the world is a smaller place and (**7**) .... people have the same type of clothes – jeans, for example, are international.

However, people (**8**) .... like to choose different clothes to (**9**) .... at different times. There are special clothes for work and sport – a business suit looks wrong on a beach and (**10**) .... puts on a T-shirt and shorts to go to the office. Policemen and nurses have uniforms (**11**) .... people can then see what (**12**) .... job is. People in hot countries can put on light clothes, but in cold places, people (**13**) .... always wear warm things like heavy sweaters and coats.

Example:

0 A is	**B** was	**C** were	*Answer:*	**0**	A B C ☐■☐	

6	**A** on	**B** in	**C** at
7	**A** many	**B** much	**C** lots
8	**A** still	**B** ever	**C** yet
9	**A** wearing	**B** wear	**C** wore
10	**A** somebody	**B** everybody	**C** nobody
11	**A** but	**B** because	**C** or
12	**A** their	**B** they	**C** them
13	**A** may	**B** must	**C** could

© Cambridge University Press, 2005

Writing Part 7

Questions 1–10

Complete this letter.
Write ONE word for each space.

Example: | **0** | *are*

Dear Christina,

How (**0**) .... you? I'm going to have (**1**) .... first horse-riding lesson tomorrow and I'm really pleased (**2**) .... it! Mum's going to drive me to the riding school (**3**) .... I can't get there by bus. The riding school is bigger (**4**) .... the one you go to. They've got over thirty horses so I (**5**) .... ride a different one next week (**6**) .... I want to.

I've got a new (**7**) .... of riding trousers and a hard hat, (**8**) .... I need to buy boots. For tomorrow's lesson I'm going to borrow (**9**) .... and see how they feel. How (**10**) .... did your boots cost? Write and tell me soon.

Love,

Maggie

Listening Part 4

Questions 1–5

You will hear a girl asking about a film club.

Listen and complete questions **1–5**.

You will hear the conversation twice.

INTERNATIONAL FILM CLUB

For people aged:	**0**	Over 15
Day of club:	**1**	
Time club opens:	**2**	
Cost for one month:	**3**	£...
Ask for:	**4**	Jon...
Club is next to the:	**5**	

Test 2 Key

Reading Part 2

Answers

1 B   2 C   3 C   4 B   5 A

Reading Part 5

Answers

6 C	8 A	10 C	12 A
7 A	9 B	11 B	13 B

Writing Part 7

Answers

1 my/the	6 if
2 about	7 pair
3 because/as	8 but
4 than	9 some/boots
5 can/could	10 much

Listening Part 4

Answers

1 Friday	3 £15	5 bus station
2 7.30	4 Kalkowitz	

Recording script and answers

Listening Part 4

You will hear a girl asking about a film club. Listen and complete questions 1 to 5. You will hear the information twice.

Man: International Film Club.

Girl: Hello. I'd like some information about the club, please.

Man: Certainly. First of all, you must be over 15. Is that OK?

Girl: Yes, that's fine – I'm 16. When are you open?

Man: When we started we opened on a Saturday but we changed the day to <u>Friday</u> – we get more people now.

Girl: Oh, OK. What about times?

Man: We open the doors at <u>seven thirty</u> and the film usually starts at seven forty-five. We close at eleven pm.

Girl: Is it expensive?

Man: It costs £7.50 to see each film, or you can pay for a month which is cheaper – <u>£15</u>.

Girl: That sounds good. What do I need to do now?

Man: Why don't you come along this week? Ask for me – my name's Jon Kalkowitz – that's <u>K-A-L-K-O-W-I-T-Z</u>.

Girl: Great. And where are you?

Man: We're in the local library building – it's next to the <u>bus station</u>.

Girl: OK. That's fine. See you this week. Thanks.

Now listen again.

(The recording is repeated.)

9 Travel

<table>
<tr><td colspan="2">9.1 Making holiday plans</td></tr>
<tr><td>Listening</td><td>Listening for specific information</td></tr>
<tr><td>Grammar</td><td>The future with going to</td></tr>
<tr><td>Pronunciation</td><td>/h/</td></tr>
<tr><td>Exam skills</td><td>Reading Part 3: Functional English</td></tr>
<tr><td colspan="2">9.2 Looking into the future</td></tr>
<tr><td>Reading</td><td>Reading for specific information</td></tr>
<tr><td>Grammar</td><td>The future with will</td></tr>
<tr><td>Spelling</td><td>Words ending in -y</td></tr>
<tr><td>Exam skills</td><td>Writing Part 7: Cloze</td></tr>
<tr><td colspan="2">Preparation</td></tr>
<tr><td colspan="2">Make one copy of the Holiday Island map on page 121 for each group of four to five students for the Extension activity in 9.1.</td></tr>
</table>

9.1 Making holiday plans

SB pages 57–58

1 Ask students to work in pairs to discuss if any of the types of holiday in the photos appeals to them and what their idea of a perfect holiday would be.

Listening

2 Play the recording and ask students to match the people with the places and the types of holiday. Then play it again and ask them to listen for how each person is going to travel.

Answers
1 Julia   Australia   beach
2 Daniel   Switzerland   walking
3 Simon   France   camping
4 Natalie   Greece   sailing
5 Julia – by plane and car
6 Daniel – by motorbike
7 Simon – by car
8 Natalie – by boat

Recording script

Daniel: Hi, Julia!
Julia: Daniel! Hi, how are you?
Daniel: I'm fine. I hear you're on holiday next week – are you going to go to Florida again?
Julia: No, Australia this time. A friend from work has a flat by a beautiful beach. We're going to fly to Sydney and then drive along the coast to the flat. What about you?
Daniel: I'm going to do some walking in Switzerland. I did ask a friend to come with me but he's decided to stay at home this year – he wants to save enough money to buy a car. So, I'm going to be all alone. I'm going to go on my motorbike. Oh, there's Natalie and Simon. We're just talking about holidays. Are you planning anything, Simon?
Simon: Hi! I'm going to go camping with my family again. I stupidly offered to drive them all down to the south of France and help them put up the tent. My friends are all planning to go to Florida, so I'm not very happy, I can tell you!
Daniel: What about you, Natalie?
Natalie: My brother has asked me to go with him to Greece. We're going to hire a boat and then sail around the Greek islands for three whole weeks! I can't wait!
Daniel, Simon and Julia: Sounds amazing! Really good! etc.

Grammar

Refer the class to the grammar explanation. Put the time line on the board and give some other examples:

Yesterday I decided to go to the cinema on (today's date). Tonight I'm going to go to the cinema.

Check that students understand that when the verb we want to use is already *go*, then we sometimes just say, for example, *I'm going to the café at lunchtime.* This is the present continuous form, which is also used for talking about the future, but more for already completed arrangements than plans. Sometimes there is very little difference in meaning:
I'm washing my hair tonight.
I'm going to wash my hair tonight.
But there can sometimes be a small difference:
I'm having caviar and champagne for dinner. (They're in the fridge.)
I'm going to have caviar and champagne at the weekend. (This is the plan.)

3 Invite students to work in pairs to ask and answer questions about the pictures.

> **Suggested answers**
> **2** He's going (to go) swimming / dive into the pool.
> **3** They're going to play tennis.
> **4** He's going to buy/have/eat an ice cream.
> **5** They're going to have a pizza.
> **6** She's going (to go) cycling.

4

> **Answers**
> **2** is going to telephone
> **3** are going to do
> **4** am going to book
> **5** is going to visit
> **6** is/are going to close
> **7** are going to meet
> **8** are/'re going to have

E xtension activity

Students should form groups of four or five. Give each group one copy of the holiday island map on page 121. The group is going to make a perfect holiday island. They can mark on the map any of the following:
hotels (how many is up to the group)
tennis courts
swimming pools
beaches
restaurants
clubs
a museum / historical site
the airport
shops / shopping centre
banks
golf course
plus anything else they think is necessary

After they have finished their discussion and completed the map, ask them to write a short description of the island for the Travel section of a newspaper. They could do this for homework.

Pronunciation

5 Ask the class to underline the words in the exercise which contain the sound /h/ as in *hand*. Play the recording so they can check their answers.

Recording script and answers

The words which contain the sound /h/ are:
hand, holiday, home, hill, how, happy, hotel

The words which don't include the sound /h/ are:
why, when, honest, hour, school

6 Ask the class to work in pairs to put the words in each sentence in the right order. They should then listen to the recording to check their answers.

Recording script and answers

1 He has a holiday home in the hills.
2 Helen hopes she'll get a horse for her birthday.
3 Help him with his homework.
4 Have a happy holiday!
5 I'm going to hire a boat and have fun.
6 Help me into the helicopter!

7 Ask the class to listen to the recording and underline the word they hear in each pair.

Recording script and answers

1 high	**3** it	**5** air	**7** art
2 hold	**4** and	**6** hall	

Reading

8 KET Reading Part 3

This exercise gives more practice for Reading Part 3. Stella has gone to a travel agent to book a holiday. Ask students to work in pairs and discuss which of the sentences A–H would best fit in gaps 1–5. They should also discuss why the three extra sentences do not fit and talk about when they could be used.

> **Answers**
> **1** C   **2** A   **3** G   **4** E   **5** B

9.2 Looking into the future
SB pages 58–59

Ask a member of the class to read the facts aloud. Ask the class what they think about these facts. Suggested questions:

Do you think $20 million is too much to pay?

Why do you think Dennis Tito went in a Russian spacecraft? (NASA refused to take a tourist.)

Are you surprised that there are 6,000 people waiting to go into space on holiday?

1 Explain that in this lesson you are going to be using the future simple tense – *will* and *won't*:
will + verb
won't / will not + verb

Check that everyone understands the vocabulary and then go through the first two or three reasons as a class. Possible answers are given below, but it is envisaged that the class will use simple sentences to answer. If these are put up on the board, they can then decide how to join them. For example:

The journey will take too long.
People won't want to go.
> People won't want to go because the journey will take too long.

Possible answers

the journey:	People won't want to go because the journey will take a long time.
the scenery:	People will go because the scenery will be fantastic.
the food:	People won't want to go there for the food.
the weather:	People won't be interested in the weather on the Moon.
the activities/ attractions:	People will like the zero gravity and will be able to do lots of interesting activities.
the accommodation:	The hotels will be interesting and modern.
the price:	It will be very expensive so people will probably not be able to afford to go.

Reading

2 Tell the class that the article is about companies who are hoping to build hotels and activity centres in space. The class should read the article and then do the exercise that follows. There is an example to help them.

Pre-teach any vocabulary that you think may cause your class difficulties.

Answers
2 How many people will (be able to) stay at the hotel?
3 How high will the holiday centre be above the Earth?
4 When will the centre be ready?
5 What will tourists be able to do at the centre?
6 How much will a trip cost?
7 Where will most of the hotel on the moon be?

Grammar

Go through the examples in the grammar explanation. Ask the class to grade the four adverbs.

definitely/certainly	100%
probably	70%
possibly	40%

3 Ask a couple of members of the class to say a sentence about each of the topics. Ask the class to write some sentences for themselves on the given topics, predicting what will happen in the future.

S pelling spot

4 Read through the explanation and check everyone understands. Ask the class to work through the exercise.

Answers

2 plays	5 monkeys	8 stays
3 happier	6 studying	9 families
4 keys	7 enjoyed	10 buys

5 **KET Writing Part 7**

Ask the class to read through the email. Ask them:
Where is Susie staying?
How does she feel?
What is she going to do tonight?

In the exam, candidates do not have a choice of words to fill the spaces with. They are given an open cloze, that is, a text with ten spaces which they have to fill. The exercise here is to get students used to dealing with a cloze.

Answers

2 a	5 but	8 there
3 am going to	6 its	9 some
4 is	7 can	10 will

E xtension activity

Ask students each to write a postcard to a friend from a holiday destination which they don't name. Walk round the class introducing vocabulary as necessary. When they have finished writing, ask a few students to read out what they have written and the class have to guess where each student has been on holiday.

Example:
I'm having a lovely time here. It is very hot and tomorrow I'm going to a famous theme park where there are dolphins and rollercoasters and also film studios. The beaches are wonderful! We went to see some alligators yesterday.
Love
Answer: Florida – Disneyworld at Orlando

Activity

Explain that the class should look at the questionnaire on page 129 of their Student's Book. Ask them to predict what kind of traveller they will be: *World Traveller*, *Happy Tourist* or *Stay-at-Home*.

Invite them to work through the questionnaire by themselves and then to turn to page 130 to work out their score. They should then form pairs and compare answers.

Exam folder 5

Speaking Parts 1 and 2

SB pages 60–61

Refer students to the Exam advice.

Part 1

1 Play the recording and explain that the class will hear an interview which will include the type of questions that are asked in the exam.

The first time they listen they should just relax and get a feel for the exam. The second time the students should fill in the chart with information from the recording.

Answers	
Name:	Pilar Martinez
Town/country:	Madrid, Spain
Favourite subject(s):	English
Free time activities:	shopping, going out with friends, cinema
Countries visited:	England, France, Portugal

Recording script

Examiner: Good morning.
Candidate: Good morning.
Examiner: What's your name?
Candidate: My name is Pilar Martinez.
Examiner: How do you spell your surname?
Candidate: My surname is M-A-R-T-I-N-E-Z.
Examiner: And where do you come from?
Candidate: I come from Madrid, in Spain.
Examiner: Where do you study?
Candidate: I study at a local school here in Madrid.
Examiner: And which subjects do you study?
Candidate: I ... I study English and History and Literature.
Examiner: Which subject do you like best?
Candidate: I like best English.
Examiner: Why do you like it?
Candidate: I like it because I enjoy learning languages, and because it will be useful when I start work.
Examiner: What do you do in your free time?
Candidate: In my free time I go shopping, I ... I like going out with my friends and ... and watching films at the cinema.
Examiner: What are you going to do next weekend?
Candidate: Next weekend it's it's my friend's birthday and she is having a big party.
Examiner: Have you ever been to other countries?
Candidate: Yes, as well as England, I have been to France and to Portugal.
Examiner: Thank you.

2 Invite the students to work in pairs, asking and answering the questions.

> **Possible questions and answers**
> How do you spell your surname? It's R-O-S-S-I-N-I .
> Where do you come from? I come from Milan.
> Where do you study? At a college.
> What subjects do you study? I study English, Maths, Italian, Art and History.
> Which subject do you like best? I like English best / I prefer English.
> Where do you usually go on holiday? / Where will you go on holiday? I usually go to the seaside.
> What are you doing / going to do next weekend? Next weekend, I'm going shopping with some friends.
> Have you (ever) been to other countries? Yes, I've been to France and Spain.

Part 2

3 Candidate B should look at page 131 of the Student's Book. Candidate B should ask A some questions about the holiday centre at Westcliffe on Sea. Candidate A should use the information given to answer the questions.

> **Holiday centre – possible questions and answers**
> B: Where is it?
> A: It's in/at Westcliffe on Sea.
> B: What can I do there?
> A: You can go swimming and play tennis.
> B: How much is it for an adult? / How much does it cost for an adult? / What's the price for an adult?
> A: It's £400 for a week in July.
> B: Is it open all year?
> A: No, only from March to November
> B: Is there a place to eat? / Can I eat there?
> A: Yes, there's an excellent restaurant.

4 The candidates change roles with B having the information and A asking the questions. Candidate A should look at page 132 of the Student's Book.

> **Burford Arts cinema – possible questions and answers**
> A: What can I see at the Arts cinema?
> B: You can see/watch an adventure film. / You can see *The Return of the Martians*.
> A: What time does the cinema open? / When does the cinema open?
> B: It opens at 2.00 pm.
> A: Can I eat there?
> B: Yes, you can eat at the Riverside Café.
> A: What is the address? / Where is it?
> B: It's 68 Helman Street, Burford.
> A: How much is a student ticket? / How much does a student ticket cost?
> B: It's £5.00.

10 Places and buildings

10.1 Inside the home	
Vocabulary	Furniture; materials; adjectives – opposites
Spelling	Words ending in -f and -fe
Exam skills	Listening Part 2: Matching Reading Part 2: Lexical multiple choice

10.2 Famous buildings	
Pronunciation	Dates in years
Grammar	The passive

Preparation

For the Activity in 10.2, photocopy the cards on page 122 and cut them up so that there are enough cards for each pair of students to have about 10 cards.

10.1 Inside the home

SB pages 62–63

Vocabulary

1 Ask students to look at the picture of a teenager's bedroom and match the vocabulary items 1–15 with the letters a–o in the pictures.

> **Answers**
>
> | | | | | | | | |
> |---|---|---|---|---|---|---|---|
> | 2 | c | 6 | l | 10 | n | 14 | g |
> | 3 | e | 7 | j | 11 | k | 15 | a |
> | 4 | i | 8 | o | 12 | b | | |
> | 5 | f | 9 | m | 13 | d | | |

2 Ask the class to work in pairs. They should talk about their own rooms at home. Point out the colours in the book and also the examples in the speech bubbles.

S pelling spot

3

> **Answers**
>
> 2 I have *some bookshelves* in my room.
> 3 *The knives are* on the table.
> 4 *The roofs are* red.
> 5 *Their wives are* in the kitchen.
> 6 I found *some leaves* on the floor.

Listening

4 Ask students to look at the objects 1–6 in their books and the names of the rooms. They should talk with a partner about which room they would expect to find the objects in. For example, in their house or flat do they have a mirror in the bedroom or the bathroom, or maybe in both?

5 **KET Listening Part 2**

In Part 2 of the Listening paper candidates must listen to identify key information. They hear an informal conversation and have to match five items with a choice of eight items.

Ask the class to read through the exercise and check they understand the vocabulary and what they have to do.

> **Answers**
>
> 1 D 2 F 3 H 4 A 5 B

Recording script

Lisa: Hi, Tom!
Tom: Oh hi, Lisa! How's the new flat?
Lisa: It's great! But we haven't finished moving all our furniture yet. The <u>metal desk</u> from my old room is <u>still in the garage</u> with lots of other things!
Tom: Did you have any problems when you moved?
Lisa: A few. The <u>leather sofa</u> was too big for the living room so it's in the <u>dining room</u> for now.
Tom: What's your new <u>bedroom</u> like?
Lisa: It's bigger than my old one and I can have the <u>computer in there</u> now. We had it in the corner of the kitchen before. My parents have put the <u>CD player in their room</u>, but they said I could have one for my birthday!
Tom: Great! What about that <u>large mirror</u> you had in the kitchen? Have you still got it?
Lisa: Yes, and it looks really good <u>in the new bathroom</u>. And do you remember my mum's books? Well, she now has <u>new bookshelves</u> in <u>the hall</u> – it's much better than the books being in their bedroom! Why don't you come and see us this evening?
Tom: That'd be great. I'll do that.

Vocabulary

6 Students can work through the pictures in pairs or as a class exercise.

> **Answers**
> the CD – plastic
> the sweater – wool
> the bag – leather
> the credit card – plastic
> the curtains – cotton
> the necklace – gold
> the window – glass and wood/plastic
> the book – paper
> the TV – glass, metal and plastic
> the watch – silver, metal, glass
> the vase – glass
> the bowl – wood

Ask the class to look around the classroom and talk about what the objects they have around them are made of.

E xtension activity

Ask the class to work in pairs or small groups – possibly single sex. They should have one piece of clean A4 paper and on it they should design the perfect bedroom. They should discuss their ideas, saying, for example:
Where shall we put the bed?
We could put the TV on a shelf.
Let's put the DVD player in the corner.
After 15–20 minutes they should present their bedroom to the rest of the class.

Useful language
in the middle/corner of the room
on the wall
at the side of the room
at the top/bottom of the wall
between the door and the window
over the bed
under the table
on the table
by / next to the bed

7 Ask students to work in pairs.

> **Answers**
>
> | | |
> |---|---|
> | narrow | wide |
> | big | little |
> | new | old |
> | cold | hot |
> | expensive | cheap |
> | high | low |
> | noisy | quiet |
> | soft | hard |
> | long | short |
> | double | single |

8 KET Reading Part 2

This exercise can be done in class or for homework. When they have finished, students should compare their answers with another student and discuss why the other adjectives are wrong.

> **Answers**
> 1 B 2 C 3 A 4 A 5 B

10.2 Famous buildings
SB pages 64–65

1 Invite students to look at the photos. They should talk about which they like best, where the buildings are, who built them and when they were built. Make sure they know how to pronounce the dates. (More work is done on dates in exercise 2.)

> **Answers**
>
> | | | |
> |---|---|---|
> | Sydney Opera House | 1959–73 | Jørn Utzon |
> | The Guggenheim Museum, Bilbao | 1997 | Frank Gehry |
> | The Eiffel Tower, Paris | 1887–9 | Gustav Eiffel |
> | The Colosseum, Rome | AD 70–82 | Vespasian |
> | The Parthenon, Athens | 447–432 BC | Pericles |
> | The Sagrada Familia, Barcelona | 1884–present | Antonio Gaudí |
>
> This building continues to be built by others since Gaudí's death.

Pronunciation

2 Ask the class to write the dates given as words. Then play the recording so they can check their answers.

> **Recording script and answers**
>
> 1 twelve ninety-two
> 2 fifteen sixty-nine
> 3 seventeen eighteen
> 4 eighteen ninety
> 5 nineteen sixty-three

3 Students write the dates as numbers this time. Pause the recording if they need extra time.

> **Recording script and answers**
>
> 1 1340
> 2 1519
> 3 1630
> 4 1780
> 5 1870

Grammar

Go through the grammar explanation in the Student's Book with the class. Refer them also to the Grammar folder on page 141 of the Student's Book. There is an extra exercise there they can do in class or for homework.

Explain that we use the passive when:
– we don't know who did something
– what happened is more important than who did it. If we want to say who did it we use *by* + the person's name.
For example:
My bag was stolen. (We don't know who by.)
The Eiffel Tower was built by Eiffel. (The building is more important than the person.)

4

> **Answers**
> 2 was/is made   6 were built
> 3 are borrowed   7 are taught
> 4 was painted   8 was bought
> 5 was sold

5 Ask students to comment on the photo of the London Eye. Has anyone been on it? What do they think it would be like? Would they like to go on it?

Ask them to work through the exercise. It might be helpful at this stage to demonstrate on the board the difference between the active and passive as this is what is tested here.

> **Answers**
> 1 was designed   7 worked
> 2 was organised   8 was built
> 3 wanted   9 was developed
> 4 are carried / can be carried   10 made
> 5 designed   11 were made
> 6 built   12 was produced

6 This exercise gives practice in making questions in the passive.

> **Answers**
> 2 When was the competition organised?
>   It was organised in 1994.
> 3 How many people are carried / does it carry / can be carried on it?
>   800 people can be carried on it.
> 4 Where was the wheel developed?
>   It was developed in the Netherlands.
> 5 Where were the capsules made?
>   They were made in the French Alps.
> 6 Who produced the glass?
>   It was produced in Italy.

E xtension activity

Ask the class to prepare a quiz for homework. Each student should prepare five questions and the answers to bring back to ask the class. There should be a mixture of dates/people/places. For example:

Neil Armstrong went to the moon in
A 1969.   **B** 1956.   **C** 1971.

The Pyramids were built by
A the Greeks.   **B** the Egyptians.   **C** the Libyans.

Activity

Photocopy page 122 of the Teacher's Book and cut it up into separate cards. You should make enough cards for each pair of students to have about ten cards each.

Invite students to work in pairs. Give each pair a pile of cards face down. Each player takes it in turns to pick up a card and say what the two things on it have in common. They must use the passive.

Suggested answers	
rice/noodles	They are both eaten in China.
cola/coffee	They are both drunk in the USA.
hamburgers/hotdogs	They are both eaten with bread / enjoyed all over the world.
cars/cameras	They are both made of metal / were both invented over 100 years ago.
Rolls Royce cars / Ferrari cars	They are both made for / driven by rich people.
watches/chocolate	They are both made in Switzerland.
diamonds/gold	They are both found in the ground / used for rings/jewellery.
a bag/shoes	They are both made of leather.
a newspaper / a magazine	They are both made of paper / read by people.
a packet of biscuits / a carton of juice	They are both bought in supermarkets.
The English language/ The Hindi language	They are both spoken in India.
Romeo and Juliet/ Hamlet	They were both written by Shakespeare.
bananas/sugar	They are both grown in the Caribbean.
horses/bicycles	They are both ridden by people.
a tie / trousers	They are both worn by men.
football / basketball	They are both played in teams.
My house/ Buckingham Palace	They are both built of brick/stone.

Reading Part 4 Right, Wrong, Doesn't say

SB pages 66–67

Ask students to read the information about this part of the Reading and Writing paper. Refer them to the Exam advice. Check they understand what they have to do.

Ask the class to look at the example of the OMR answer sheet, where they need to record their answers in the exam. They should be reminded that it is very important to record the right answer on the right line as it is very easy to 'jump' a line in the exam and lose marks.

Background information

George Hearst was a rich miner and he bought 40,000 acres of land in 1865. In 1919 his only son, William Randolph Hearst, inherited the land, now nearly 250,000 acres.

Part 4

Ask the class to read the text to get a general idea of what it is about. A few preliminary questions can be asked at this time:

Who built the castle?   *William Randolph Hearst*
When was the castle built?   *1922–1939*
How much did it cost?   *$30 million*
When did Hearst die?   *1951*

The class should read through the text again and look carefully at the examples 0, 00 and 000. There is only one example in the actual exam.

Ask the class to work through the text and do the exam task. The questions are in the order in which the answers occur in the text.

Answers						
21 B	22 B	23 A	24 C	25 A	26 C	27 B

11 Sport

11.1 Living for sport

Vocabulary	Sports and sports equipment
Listening	Identifying gist meaning
Pronunciation	/b/ and /v/
Exam skills	Reading Parts 3 and 4: Multiple-choice questions
Grammar extra	Word order in questions

11.2 Keeping fit

Grammar	Verbs in the -ing form
Exam skills	Listening Part 5: Note taking
	Writing Part 6: Spelling
Spelling	gu- , qu-

Preparation

Make a copy of the recording script on page 123 for each student. This will be used in 11.2.

11.1 Living for sport

SB pages 68–69

1 Refer students to the photos and ask them to discuss the questions in pairs or small groups for two minutes. Then elicit their ideas.

Vocabulary

2 Suggest that students make lists for each sport.

> **Answers**
> *snowboarding:* boots, board, gloves
> *baseball:* ball, bat, boots, glove
> *windsurfing:* board, gloves, sail
> *tennis:* ball, court, net, racket
> *basketball:* ball, basket, court, net

3 Explain that it is not important for students to understand every word in these recordings. Play each recording twice if necessary.

Answers

	sport	play/do or watch?
Speaker 1	tennis	play
Speaker 2	basketball	watch
Speaker 3	baseball	watch
Speaker 4	snowboarding	do
Speaker 5	windsurfing	do

Recording script

Speaker 1: I'm doing really well this year. I bought a new racket, perhaps that's why! The main thing is I can hit the ball much harder now. I've won my last three matches.

Speaker 2: They have matches on television here every week and I sometimes go to support the college team. Last time I went, they scored twenty-nine baskets, but they still lost!

Speaker 3: Last year, I stayed in New York with my uncle and he got tickets for the Yankees. I loved every minute of the game, it was so exciting. He gave me a bat to bring home. I haven't used it. It's on my bedroom shelf!

Speaker 4: I did it for a week when the snow was very good. I'm saving for my own board now. Have you heard the joke about people like us? What's the difference between someone learning and his teacher? Answer, about three days! Well, it is easier than skiing.

Speaker 5: I had a week of lessons in Corsica. The sea was very warm there. Back in England, I have to wear a wetsuit because it's very cold and I often fall in the water!

4 Elicit the answer (football). Then ask students to find the words in the word square in pairs.

Answers

cup	match	kick
goal	boots	team
referee	net	
club	score	

e	s	t	r	i	k	e	r
a	c	u	p	b	h	o	e
n	o	t	g	o	a	l	t
e	r	e	f	e	r	e	e
t	e	c	l	u	b	k	a
m	a	t	c	h	a	i	m
o	n	l	i	r	t	c	o
b	o	o	t	s	e	k	t

Pronunciation

5 The focus is on the sounds /b/ as in *basketball* and /v/ as in *volleyball*. Draw student's attention to the pictures. Explain that it is important to pronounce these two consonants clearly, to make them sound different from each other. Play the recording twice if necessary.

6 Give students the beginning of a sentence if they have difficulty getting started. For example, *Before breakfast, I visited a very beautiful …*

Reading

7 KET Reading Parts 3 and 4

This is a training exercise, looking at multiple-choice questions. The original interview with Michael Owen appeared on the internet.

B ackground information

Michael Owen played for many years at Liverpool Football Club. He was one of their most talented strikers. He joined Real Madrid in 2004. He has also represented England at a number of events, including the 1998 World Cup and the 2000 and 2004 European Championships.

Ask students to read each question carefully and then choose the correct response.

Answers

1 B **2** C **3** C **4** B **5** A

8 Suggest students each write up to five short sentences on their own. Then write some of these on the board.

Possible answers

He first played for Liverpool when he was 17.
He was in the 1998 England team.
He is a striker.
He loves scoring goals.
He runs very quickly.

G rammar extra

Following the work on question forms in Units 1 and 2, this reminds students about word order in questions, which the *Cambridge Learner Corpus* has shown to be a problem for KET candidates. Ask students to read the information carefully before doing exercise 9.

9

Answers

2 Which team does Totti play for?
3 Have you got a snowboard?
4 When is the next World Cup?
5 Why didn't you go to the match?
6 Which is your favourite sport? / Which sport is your favourite?
7 Where does the referee come from?
8 Do you want to swim in the competition?

10 Remind students that in Part 2 of the Speaking test they will have to form questions from a card like this one.

Possible questions

When is the sports competition?
Which sports will there be?
Will the sports competition be at the college or somewhere else?
What clothes should I wear?
Are there any prizes in the competition?

11.2 Keeping fit

SB pages 70–71

1 Give students two or three minutes to discuss their views. Elicit their ideas.

2 This flow chart is taken from a British teenage magazine. Suggest students work through it in pairs.

Grammar

3 Elicit all the examples – there are ten more in all.

> **Answers**
> spend more time playing
> going out with your friends
> winning
> keep taking the lift
> walking to school
> relaxing
> exercising
> sleeping in a maths lesson
> start playing some sport
> stop exercising

4

> **Answers**
> | | | | | | |
> |---|---|---|---|---|---|
> | 1 | sitting | 4 | getting | 7 | running |
> | 2 | making | 5 | driving | 8 | throwing |
> | 3 | swimming | 6 | playing | 9 | carrying |

5 Ask students to complete the exercise and then compare answers.

> **Answers**
> | | | | | | |
> |---|---|---|---|---|---|
> | 2 | hitting | 5 | moving | 7 | practising |
> | 3 | playing | 6 | walking | 8 | winning |
> | 4 | going | | | | |

6 Encourage students to use *really*, to sound more natural. Give them a couple of minutes to talk about 1–8 in pairs. Then elicit answers round the class.

E xtension activity

Ask students to prepare a class poster covering some of their favourite (and least favourite) activities. Encourage students to bring in photos of themselves doing these activities. They should write sentences to go with the photos using -*ing* forms. For example, *Paola really loves playing beach volleyball*.

Listening

7 **KET Listening Part 5**

Remind students to check their spelling carefully. Play the recording twice.

> **P** hotocopiable recording script activity ⋯⟩ page 123

Hand out copies of the recording script after the first listening and ask students to read it as they listen again. They can then check their own answers from the script.

> **Answers**
> | | | | | |
> |---|---|---|---|---|
> | 1 | 11.15 (pm) / quarter past eleven | | 4 | Colville |
> | 2 | 88679 | | 5 | Tuesday |
> | 3 | 25 / twenty-five | | | |

Recording script

This is the 24-hour information line for the Solway Fitness Club. Our opening hours are from six thirty in the morning until eleven fifteen at night, seven days a week. If you love exercising, you'll love our club!

We have a large gym with all the latest equipment. To book an introduction to the gym, please phone Jack Bergman on 0453 88679 now.

There are two pools at the club. We have a ten-metre pool just for diving and a twenty-five metre swimming pool. Why not try relaxing in our steam room before you swim? It's fantastic!

If you'd like to become a member of Solway Fitness Club, please phone us again during working hours and ask to speak to Mrs Colville, that's C-O-L-V-I-double L-E.

We also give guided tours of the club once a week. These tours are at two fifteen every Tuesday afternoon. You don't have to book a place, but don't be late!

We hope you enjoy getting fit at Solway Fitness Club!

S pelling spot

The *Cambridge Learner Corpus* shows that students sometimes omit the *u*, especially after *g*.

8

> **Answers**
> | | | | | | |
> |---|---|---|---|---|---|
> | 1 | quickly | 3 | guitar | 5 | quiet |
> | 2 | quarter | 4 | guest | 6 | guess |

9 **KET Writing Part 6**

All the words in this KET Part 6 task are -*ing* forms.

> **Answers**
> | | | | | | |
> |---|---|---|---|---|---|
> | 1 | skiing | 3 | fishing | 5 | sailing |
> | 2 | cycling | 4 | climbing | | |

Activity

This activity offers further practice of -*ing* forms. Before students start, get them to discuss as a class how to organise the survey. For example, different groups could find out the answer to each of the four questions. Make sure students spend enough time planning the survey and preparing the questions.

Writing folder 3

Writing Part 9　Short message

SB pages 72–73

There are two kinds of Part 9 task: 'with input' and 'instructions only'. This covers the 'with input' and Writing folder 5 covers the 'instructions only' type.

Ask students to read the information about this part of the Reading and Writing paper. Explain that it is very important for them to include *all three* pieces of information in their answer.

1　These KET answers have been taken from the *Cambridge Learner Corpus*. Ask students to correct the answers in pairs, following the instructions in the bulleted points.

> **Corrected answers**
>
> **1**
> I'm going to visit your town next Friday. I'd like to visit the sports club near your house. I think it's a very nice place. Meet me at 7 p.m.
> Yours,
>
> **2**
> I think that the most interesting place near my town is a little lake, because it's not noisy there and there are a lot of animals. You can drive to it.
> Love,
>
> **3**
> Let's meet in front of the football ground at 17.00. I want to buy a camera and a computer game. See you on Saturday.
>
> **4**
> Hello,
> I have a basketball, a football, a computer and a television to sell. The basketball and football are almost new. I've only played with them once. I've had the computer and television for six months but I want to sell them.
> Bye,

2　Elicit an answer quickly: all four answers need to be signed (see introduction).

3　Ask students to decide on the three pieces of information in pairs.

> **Answer**
> 1 information about the pool
> 2 how to get there
> 3 the best time to swim

4　Elicit answers to the three questions students were asked to think about before asking students to decide on the better answer.

> **Answer**
> Answer B is better, because it is the right length and includes all the necessary information.
> At only 20 words, answer A would lose one mark out of five. It also fails to include information about how to get to the pool from the town centre, so would only score three out of five.

5　Elicit ideas on the information that is needed and then ask students to rewrite answer A, including their ideas.

> **Possible answer**
> Hi Alex,
> There's a swimming pool near the motorway. It's really big and has a nice café, too. Why not go at lunchtime or on Saturday? You can take tram 14 from the town centre. It stops outside the pool.
> See you,
> Mario

6　Ask students to do the exercise in pairs.

> **Answers**
>
> | | | | |
> |---|---|---|---|
> | B 1 | D 3 | F 1 | H 2 |
> | C 2 | E 1 | G 3 | |

7　Encourage students to use their own words and different ideas in their answers. They can do this for homework.

> **Sample answer**
> Dear Alex,
> Our pool is lovely! It's big and there are two water rides. Why not go in the afternoon, when it's quieter? You can catch a bus or walk there. It's not too far. Have fun!
> Love,
> Ellie

12 The family

12.1 Family trees	
Vocabulary	People in a family
Exam skills	Listening Part 3: Multiple choice
Grammar extra	Possessive adjectives and pronouns
Pronunciation	Vowel sounds /aʊ/ and /ɔ:/
Spelling	Words ending in -le

12.2 Large and small	
Exam skills	Reading Part 4: Right, Wrong, Doesn't say
Grammar	Subject, object and reflexive pronouns Pronouns *everything*, *anything*, *nothing*, etc.

12.1 Family trees
SB pages 74–75

Vocabulary

Background information

Scarlett Johansson has starred in some very successful films, including *Lost in Translation* and *The Girl with a Pearl Earring*.

1 Ask if students have seen any of Scarlett Johansson's films. Suggest they spend two minutes reading her bio text and completing the family tree.

> **Answers**
> 1 grandfather 3 mother 5 sister
> 2 father 4 (older) brother

2

> **Answers**
> 1 uncle 4 grandmother 6 granddaughter
> 2 aunt 5 grandson 7 grandchild
> 3 cousin

3 Ask students to make a simple family tree, similar to the one in exercise 1. They should write in the names of their family members and their relationship to them, for example *father*, *brother*.

Listening

4 **KET Listening Part 3**

Play the recording twice and then elicit answers.

> **Answers**
> 1 C 2 B 3 C 4 A 5 B

Recording script

Nick: Hello, Nick speaking.
Helen: Hi, it's your cousin, Helen.
Nick: How are you?
Helen: Fine. I'm ringing about Granddad's 70th birthday party. Will it be on Friday 26th, or Saturday 27th September?
Nick: Actually, Mum and Uncle Jack decided on Sunday 28th because several people couldn't do Saturday or Friday.
Helen: OK. Are you going to have the party at your house?
Nick: It's too small! There's a nice room at his golf club, so we'll have it there. There's lunch before the party, at Mario's restaurant.
Helen: Great. Will the party still start at three thirty?
Nick: No, four. We'll finish eating around two forty-five and it's an hour's drive.
Helen: Mm. I can take you there in my car.
Nick: Thanks, but I'll have mine. Why don't you take Aunt Rose, Uncle Jack's sister from Australia?
Helen: Fine. Now, what about presents? My brother's going to buy Granddad a box set of three CDs, and there's a beautiful mirror I'd like to get for him. What do you think?
Nick: Sounds excellent. I've bought him a leather suitcase.
Helen: He'll love that. Well, see you on the day then, Nick.
Nick: Yes. Bye, Helen.

Grammar extra

5 Check whether students already know these possessive adjectives and pronouns, which they should use in the speaking practice when talking about their family trees.

Pronunciation

6 The focus is on the sounds /aʊ/ as in *cow* and /ɔ:/ as in *draw*. Draw students' attention to the pictures. These sounds are often confused and the words mis-spelled.

Ask students to write the words from the box in either group 1 or group 2. Then play the recording for them to check if they were right. Play it again and ask them to repeat the words.

S pelling spot

7 Ask students to do the exercise on their own and then compare answers.

Answers					
1 castle		**3** apple		**5** little	
2 bicycle		**4** single		**6** people	

12.2 Large and small
SB pages 76–77

1 Ask students to discuss their views and then elicit answers. The picture shows the Hayden family, featured in the Reading section that follows. There are seven children in this family.

2 This provides further practice of *-ing* forms.

Possible answers	
being by yourself	having a low supermarket bill
keeping the place tidy	travelling cheaply

Reading

3 **KET Reading Part 4**

Suggest students underline the relevant words.

Answer
Sam is close to Michael. (*get on quite well ... because he is kind and helps me*)

4 Ask students to skim the text to find out who Joe gets on well with.

Answer
Joe gets on well with Michael and David.

5 Remind students that if there is no information in the text, they will need to choose C, 'Doesn't say'. When eliciting answers, ask students to look at the relevant parts of the text, especially for the C answers, 3, 5 and 7.

Answers					
2 B	**3** C	**4** B	**5** C	**6** A	**7** C

E xtension activity

Ask the class for their views on Naomi Hayden's position as the youngest in the family and the only girl. Then ask them to write a paragraph about Naomi, based on what they have just discussed.

Grammar

6

Answers		
subject pronouns	*object pronouns*	*reflexive pronouns*
I	me	myself
you	you	yourself
he, she, it	him, her, it	himself, herself, itself
we	us	ourselves
you	you	yourselves
they	them	themselves

7 Explain that *everybody* has exactly the same meaning as *everyone*, and similarly *anybody – anyone* and *nobody – no one*.

Answers	
things	*people*
something	somebody / someone
anything	anybody / anyone
everything	everybody / everyone
nothing	nobody / no one

8

Answers	
2 Somebody/Someone	**6** everything
3 anything	**7** everybody/everyone
4 something	**8** anybody/anyone
5 nobody/no one	

9 This exercise can be set for homework if time is short. Note that relative pronouns are not actually tested at KET, though they may appear in texts.

Answers					
1 who	**3** which	**5** which			
2 who	**4** who	**6** which			

Activity

Suggest students form groups of four or five to discuss how to spend the day.

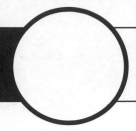

Units 9–12 Revision

SB pages 78–79

This revision unit recycles the language and topics from Units 9–12, as well as providing exam practice for Reading Part 2 and training for Writing Part 9.

Speaking

1 Ask students to work on their own matching the questions and replies. Elicit answers. Then ask students to work in pairs, taking it in turn to answer the questions. Encourage them to use their own ideas and give full answers.

Grammar

2

> **Answers**
> 1 I enjoyed *seeing* your family.
> 2 I will *wait for you* at the station.
> 3 This is the best book for *learning* English.
> 4 I think *it* will cost £30.
> 5 You don't need to ask *anybody*.
> 6 I don't mind *getting* the bus to your place.
> 7 We can ride horses and we can *fish / go fishing* in the lake.
> 8 If anybody *is* interested, call this number.
> 9 You can *come* to London by train.
> 10 The village is famous because it *was* built *by* three Roman emperors.

3

> **Answers**
> 2 was taken
> 3 was shown
> 4 was worn
> 5 was written
> 6 is known

Vocabulary

4

> **Answers**
> 1 match   4 goalkeeper   7 net
> 2 teams   5 gloves   8 scored
> 3 players   6 kicked   9 referee

5 Explain that there may be more than one answer, depending on students' ideas.

> **Possible answers**
> 1 cousin (because a cousin could be male or female)
> 2 desk (because everything else can go on the wall)
> 3 wardrobe (because the other three are made of material of some kind)
> 4 grey (because it has no red in it)
> 5 golf (because it is not played on the water)
> 6 silver (because it is not a kind of material, but an example of a metal)

6

> **Answers**
> 1 C   2 B   3 B   4 A   5 B

Writing

7 Ask students to correct the punctuation and compare answers. Then ask them to decide which three questions go with each answer.

> **Corrected emails**
> **A**
> I'd love to come sailing with you and your family, Andrea. I go sailing about ten times a year, so I've got something to wear. Can I borrow a life jacket?
>
> **B**
> You asked me about my room. Well, it's quite big, with two windows. From one, I can only see the street, but from the other, there's a lovely park with trees. I want some new curtains for my room.
>
> **C**
> I'm going to Sicily with my brother at Easter. We're going to spend a week by the sea and then we'll go walking near Etna. It's beautiful there.
>
> **Questions**
> Email A answers questions 3, 8 and 10.
> Email B answers questions 1, 6 and 9.
> Email C answers questions 2, 5 and 7.
> Question 4 does not match any of the emails.

Test 3

Reading Part 4

Questions 1–7

Read the article about how the modern Olympic Games started.
Are the sentences **1–7** 'Right' (**A**) or 'Wrong' (**B**)?
If there is not enough information to answer 'Right' (**A**) or 'Wrong' (**B**), choose 'Doesn't say' (**C**).

For questions **1–7**, mark **A**, **B** or **C**.

The modern Olympic Games

The first modern Olympic Games were the dream of a Frenchman called Baron de Coubertin. The Olympic Games stopped in AD 393 and de Coubertin wanted them to start again. But de Coubertin found that, in the beginning, not many people thought it was a good idea to start the Games again. Then, in June 1894, he talked at a meeting in Paris and twelve countries agreed to his idea of having the Games in Athens in 1896. Big crowds came to see about 245 men, mostly Greek, in the competitions. Many different cities around the world have had the Games since then.

The cities need time to get ready for the Games. For a start, they need to build places for people to stay. In the past, the sports people were given rooms in schools or hotels. But in 1932, at the Los Angeles Games, the first special Olympic Village was built. It was like a small city, and people didn't really have to leave it. Only men lived there. The women, 127 in all, had to sleep in a Los Angeles hotel! Nowadays, cities are given lots of time to get ready. For example, Sydney, in Australia, had seven years to get ready for the Olympics in 2000.

© Cambridge University Press, 2005

Example:

0 Baron de Coubertin came from France.

A Right   **B** Wrong   **C** Doesn't say   *Answer:* **0**   A B C

---

1 Very few people agreed with de Coubertin at first.

A Right   **B** Wrong   **C** Doesn't say

2 De Coubertin wanted the first modern Olympics to be in Paris.

A Right   **B** Wrong   . **C** Doesn't say

3 People from all over the world went to the Games in Athens.

A Right   **B** Wrong   **C** Doesn't say

4 Before 1932, sportsmen and women had to find their own places to stay.

A Right   **B** Wrong   **C** Doesn't say

5 The Los Angeles Olympic Village had most things that people needed.

A Right   **B** Wrong   **C** Doesn't say

6 In 1932, the sportsmen and women stayed in different places.

A Right   **B** Wrong   **C** Doesn't say

7 It took a long time to build the Olympic Village in Sydney.

A Right   **B** Wrong   **C** Doesn't say

Writing Part 6

Questions 1–5

Read the descriptions of some things you can find in a bedroom.
What is the word for each one?

The first letter is already there. There is one space for each other letter in the word.

Example:

0 You can sit at this and do your homework.   d _ _ _

Answer: | **0** | *desk*

---

1 This is usually made of wood and you keep   w _ _ _ _ _ _ _
your clothes inside it.

2 Look into this when you do your hair.   m _ _ _ _ _

3 You can put all your books on these.   s _ _ _ _ _ _

4 This may show your favourite band and you can   p _ _ _ _ _
have it on the wall.

5 These are by the window and are closed at night.   c _ _ _ _ _ _ _

Writing Part 9

Read this notice on a wall at your school.

YOUR FAMILY

Hi! I'm Sonia and I'm writing something for the
school newspaper on families. Can you help me?
How many brothers and sisters do you have? Are
you the youngest or the oldest in your family – or
are you a middle or an only child? What do you
most enjoy doing together as a family?

Leave me a note in Room 9. Thanks!

Write a note to Sonia. Answer all her questions.
Write **25–35** words.

Questions 1–5

You will hear some information about a football match.

Listen and complete questions **1–5**.
You will hear the information twice.

Leighton Town Football Club

Information for:	*April 12th–19th*
Day of match:	**1** _____
Time coach leaves car park:	**2** _____
For a coach seat, telephone:	**3** .... *before Monday pm*
Cost of family ticket:	**4** £ _____
Tonbridge car park at:	**5** .... *Road*

© Cambridge University Press, 2005

Test 3 Key

Reading Part 4

Answers

1 A   2 B   3 C   4 B   5 A   6 A   7 C

Writing Part 6

Answers

1 wardrobe	3 shelves	5 curtains
2 mirror	4 poster	

Writing Part 9

Sample answer

Dear Sonia,

I'm Ginetta in Class 3. I've got two older brothers and a baby sister. We really like playing volleyball together, but my sister just watches us because she's only 18 months old!

Ginetta

Listening Part 5

Answers

1 Wednesday	3 0476 76129	5 Carrow
2 5.15	4 £42.80	

Recording script

Listening Part 5

You will hear some information about a football match. Listen and complete questions 1 to 5. You will hear the information twice.

Thank you for calling Leighton Town Football Club. This information is for the week of 12th to 19th April. There is a change to our game next week. Leighton Town are now playing Tonbridge United in Tonbridge on <u>Wednesday</u> not Tuesday night.

Leighton Town will have three coaches to take people to Tonbridge to see the game. The coaches will go from the club car park at <u>five fifteen</u>. The match starts at seven thirty and the journey will take about one hour. For a seat on the coach call <u>0476 76129</u> before Monday evening.

There are still lots of tickets left for the coaches. Tickets, with entrance to the match, are £15.40 for adults and £9.50 for children. There is also a cheaper family ticket for <u>£42.80</u>. Please do not eat or drink anything on the coach. There will be time to buy snacks and drinks in Tonbridge before the game. The coaches will park at <u>Carrow</u> Road in Tonbridge – that's C-A-double R-O-W Road. Thank you.

Now listen again.

(The recording is repeated.)

13 The weather

13.1 Sun, rain or snow?	
Vocabulary	Weather
Exam skills	Listening Part 2: Multiple matching
Grammar extra	*(not) as … as*
Pronunciation	weak forms

13.2 Too much weather!	
Grammar	*enough* and *too*
Spelling	*to*, *too* and *two*
Exam skills	Reading Part 5: Multiple-choice cloze

Preparation

Make a copy of the recording script on page 124 for each student. This will be used in 13.1.

13.1 Sun, rain or snow?
SB pages 80–81

Vocabulary

1 Invite the class to look at the photos of different types of weather. Ask them to name them: *fog, cloud, snow, wind, storm, sun, rain* and put them up on the board. Ask students to make adjectives from the nouns. Check the spelling is correct.

Answers
fog – foggy
cloud – cloudy
snow – snowy
wind – windy
storm – stormy
sun – sunny
rain – rainy

Point out that when describing today's weather, if it is actually raining we usually say *It's raining* rather than *It's rainy*. *Rainy* is used to describe a period of time when it rained often. *Snowy* and *It's snowing* are also used in that way. Also introduce the idea of *wet* and *dry*. For example: *It's dry and sunny. It's cold and wet.*

The class should find the words in the word square individually, complete the sentences and then compare answers.

Answers

1 windy
2 raining
3 sunny
4 cloudy
5 wet
6 foggy
7 stormy
8 dry
9 snowy

2 In pairs, students should talk about the weather where they live. This may lead into a discussion into the hottest/coldest/driest places in the world.

Background information

Hottest place in the world – Death Valley, California, USA: average maximum temperature for July, 46°C.
Coldest place in the world – Polyus Nedostupnosti, Antarctica: annual mean temperature -58°C.
Wettest place in the world – Mawsynram, India: average annual rainfall 11,873 mm.
Windiest place in the world – Mount Washington, USA: wind speed of 371.75 km / hour recorded in 1934.
Probably Antarctica is the most consistently cold and windy place in the world.

3 Ask students to look at the map and discuss the weather for summer and winter in the places marked.

Listening

4 KET Listening Part 2

Ask students to look at the task. There is an example to help them. Play the recording twice.

Answers

1 A 2 H 3 G 4 F 5 B

Recording script

Girl: How was your trip, Dan? I'd love to go round the world.

Dan: It was great. First we went to London, but only for a few days as it rained all the time. Both of us got really wet.

Girl: You went to Paris next, didn't you?

Dan: Well, Paris wasn't at all sunny but it was better than London – a bit cloudy.

Girl: Did you go up the Eiffel Tower?

Dan: Yes, we both had a great time!

Girl: Where did you go after Paris?

Dan: To Cairo. We saw the Pyramids.

Girl: Was it very hot?

Dan: It wasn't as hot as in summer. It was quite windy actually.

Girl: I'd love to go there.

Dan: Yes, you'd like it. We went to Sydney next. We didn't get to the famous Bondi Beach as there were a lot of thunderstorms. We did do some shopping there.

Girl: I bet that was expensive!

Dan: It wasn't as expensive as Tokyo. It was hot and sunny there – no rain at all for the whole five days we were there!

Girl: And then you went to the USA, didn't you?

Dan: Yes, to San Francisco, which is famous for its fog. It was so thick we couldn't even see the Golden Gate bridge! But it was warmer than some of the other places!

Photocopiable recording script activity ⋯⟶ page 124

Hand out copies of the recording script. Play the recording again and ask students to underline where each answer comes.

Grammar extra

5 Refer students to the information on (not) as … as in their books. Ask them to talk about the weather in the different places in the chart.

Possible answers
The weather in Beijing was cloudy yesterday, the same as in Rome.
Vancouver was not as cold as Moscow.
Mexico City was hotter than Sydney.
Athens was as warm as Madrid.

Ask the class to write six similar sentences each, either in class or for homework.

Pronunciation

6 Ask the class to work through the exercise in pairs, filling in the missing words. When they have finished, play the recording and ask them to say what the missing words all have in common.

Answers

1 to	3 a	5 a	7 at
2 a	4 to	6 some	8 than

The missing words are all unstressed, weak forms with the sound /ə/.

7 In pairs the class should read through the sentences and underline the unstressed words which have the schwa sound.

Play the recording so students can check their answers.

Answers

1 a	3 to, the	5 for	7 was, a, from
2 of, them	4 for	6 to	8 some

13.2 Too much weather!

SB pages 82–83

1

Answers
1 True
2 True
3 False – The Atacama Desert has an average rainfall of 0.5 mm, although there are some parts of it where rainfall hasn't been recorded for 400 years!
4 True

Grammar

Refer students to the grammar explanation.

2 Ask the class to work in pairs and to look at the pictures and decide what each person is saying.

3 Students should match one adjective with a verb to complete a sentence. Some adjectives can be used more than once.

E xtension activity

Students should work in pairs.
Student A should write ten questions to ask Student B about a holiday he or she has been on.
Student B should write ten questions to ask Student A about a party he or she has been to.
Students take turns to answer each others' questions, trying to use *too* and *enough*.

Example questions and answers
A: What was the food like?
B: Terrible – it was too spicy / it wasn't hot enough.
A: What was the hotel like?
B: Awful – it was too far to walk to from the beach / it wasn't near enough to the beach.

B: What was the party like?
A: Terrible – there were too many people.
B: What was the music like?
A: Awful – it was too loud.

Other situations could be:
a trip to the cinema
a day at school
a shopping trip

Reading

4 **KET Reading Part 5**

The article is about a 'storm chaser' – a person in the USA who spends his/her time following storms, mainly to get photos but also often for research. Ask students to read through the text first to get an idea of what it is about. They should then look at the options and choose the best one.

S pelling spot

5 Check that students understand the differences between *to*, *too* and *two*. Ask them to give you example sentences, e.g.

to – *I'm going to school / to do my homework.*
too – *It's too hot to work today. I'm going home too.*
two – *Two ice creams, please.*

Ask them to work through the exercise.

6

Activity

The class should form four teams – one for each season. They should take it in turns to say a sentence about their season. For example:
In the winter I go skiing with my family.
My birthday is in winter and I get lots of presents.
Summer isn't as nice as winter because it is too hot for me.

Each correct sentence scores a point.

When the game is finished ask students to write a paragraph about their favourite season and say why they don't like the other seasons as much.

Exam folder 7

Listening Part 2 Multiple matching
SB pages 84–85

Ask students to read the information about this part of the
Listening paper.

1 This exercise practises the type of words that are tested
in Part 2. Ask students to write as many words as they
can in the topic sets, and give each set a title.

> **Possible answers**
>
> 2 *Months of the Year:* January, February, March, April, May,
> June, July, August, September, October, November,
> December.
>
> 3 *Sports:* football, swimming, rugby, baseball, basketball,
> volleyball, tennis, golf, athletics, hockey, skiing, skating,
> diving
>
> 4 *Colours:* blue, red, green, yellow, purple, pink, black,
> brown, white, orange, beige
>
> 5 *Clothes:* dress, jacket, trousers, jeans, blouse, T-shirt,
> pants, socks, coat, skirt, shorts, jumper, sweater
>
> 6 *Family:* aunt, sister, uncle, cousin, grandmother,
> grandfather, daughter, niece, nephew, son, father,
> mother
>
> 7 *Food:* apple, soup, burger, bread, salad, fish, chicken,
> cheese, rice, spaghetti, tomato, toast, chips

2 The first part of the exam task is reproduced so that
students can see how the distraction works. It is
important for them to realise that there are always
distractors, so they don't just write down the first word
they hear.

Part 2

Refer the class to the Exam advice, and the example of the
answer sheet, then play the recording and ask students to
do the exam task.

> **Answers**
>
> 6 B   7 G   8 A   9 F   10 C

Recording script and answers

**Listen to Penny talking to her cousin about the presents
she bought on holiday for her friends. Who got which
present? For questions 6 to 10 write a letter, A to H, next
to each person. You will hear the conversation twice.**

Penny: Hi, Nick.

Nick: Hi, Penny. How was your holiday in Switzerland?

Penny: It was great – hot and sunny every day and some
nice shops! Look, Nick, I bought you a cup. See, it's got
'Switzerland' written on it.

Nick: Oh thanks! Did you get a pen for James? He's always
taking mine.

Penny: I got him a CD of a local band – he likes anything
to do with music.

Nick: True. What about Becky? Did you get her a watch? It
might help her to be on time!

Penny: She's actually getting one for her birthday, so I got
her some nice soap – look, it's in a really lovely box.

Nick: Mm. She'll like that.

Penny: And for Alice – well Alice is difficult to buy for, but
in the end I bought her a book about skiing.

Nick: Good idea! Now, what about Tom?

Penny: He's got lots of books about Switzerland, so I
bought him a picture to put on his wall.

Nick: That leaves Lucy. You didn't get her a watch, did
you?

Penny: No, I just got her a comb. I couldn't think of
anything else.

Nick: OK. Anyway, I must go. Thanks for the cup!

Now listen again.

(The recording is repeated.)

 **Books and studying**

14.1 Something good to read

Reading	Questionnaire
	Photo story
Grammar	Position of adjectives
Pronunciation	Silent consonants
Spelling	Words that are often confused

14.2 Learn something new!

Vocabulary	School subjects
Exam skills	Listening Part 4: Note taking
	Reading Part 3: Functional language
Grammar extra	*rather than*

Preparation

Make a copy of the *When do you say this?* game board on page 125 for each pair of students. This will be used for the Extension activity in 14.2. Each pair will also need a dice.

14.1 Something good to read
SB pages 86–87

Reading

1 Ask students to work in pairs to do the questionnaire. As a round-up to this activity find out who reads most in the class and find out what type of book is the most popular.

E xtension activity

Ask the class to prepare a paragraph about a book/story/magazine they like. They should write notes and then come to class prepared to persuade a small group of students to read their favourite story.

2 Students should read through the photo story and then discuss it in pairs. Round up the activity by asking the whole class how they think the story will end.

Advantages of Julia joining the band: She's got a new electric guitar. James thinks the band needs a girl. She's got a garage to practise in.

Advantages of Ed joining the band: He plays the guitar really well and he can write songs. He lives in a large house, so there might be a possibility of practising there.

Grammar

3 Refer students to the information about the order of adjectives before a noun. It is important that they realise that there is a pre-determined order but at their level of English the main thing to remember is that opinion comes before fact.

Ask students to complete the chart with the underlined words in the photo story.

Answers

1 What's it like? opinion	2 How big? size	3 How old? age	4 What colour?	5 Where's it from? nationality	6 What kind?	NOUN
great		new			electric	guitar
	tall			American		boy
	large		white			house

4 Students should work through this exercise using the chart to check the order.

Answers
1 a boring old book
2 a colourful new magazine
3 a modern Japanese computer
4 the excellent new school library
5 the long adventure book
6 the expensive little leather bag
7 a beautiful white dress
8 a clever young writer

For more practice, refer students to the Grammar folder on page 143 of the Student's Book.

5 In pairs, students should make sentences about the topics given.

Possible answers
2 I am reading a great new thriller. It is about this brilliant American scientist who finds a way of making people invisible.
3 My favourite item of clothing is a short, blue cotton skirt which I wear to parties.
4 My best friend is a fifteen-year-old French girl. She's tall and slim and I think she's very pretty.
5 I have a small, tidy, rectangular bedroom.

Pronunciation

6

Answers					
1 w	2 k	3 h	4 h	5 t	6 w

7 Students fill in the blank with the missing silent letter. They should practise saying the words in pairs. When they have finished, play the recording so they can check the pronunciation.

Recording script and answers

1 island
2 castle
3 half
4 climb
5 autumn
6 knife
7 Wednesday
8 hour

S pelling spot

8 Students often confuse these words in the Writing part of the KET exam. Ask them to work through the exercise. They may have to make changes to the base word.

Answers
1 *By* the time she is 20 she will know *whether* she *wants* to be a doctor or a teacher.
2 The *weather* was really *bad* when I was on holiday.
3 You don't *want* to stay in *bed* all day, do you?
4 She said, '*Bye*' and went out to *buy* a book.
5 We are going to get some *things* from town.
6 I *won't* be home late tonight.

14.2 Learn something new!
SB pages 88–89

Vocabulary

1 Ask the class to work in pairs, putting the school subjects in the order they like them.

2 Students discuss what subjects they would like to do, using the illustrations as a prompt.

Listening

3 KET Listening Part 4

Students are going to hear a conversation between a girl called Sylvia and a man who works at a theatre school. They should listen and fill in the missing information.

Answers
1 November
2 (£)60
3 9.15 / a quarter past nine / nine fifteen
4 Marylebone (High Street)
5 189

Recording script

Man: Hello. Can I help you?
Sylvia: Yes, please. I'd like some information about Saturday classes at the school.
Man: I'm afraid the classes are full until the end of October. The new classes begin on <u>3rd November</u>. Can you send me a cheque and I'll keep a place for you? It's £30 for each class. Which classes are you interested in?
Sylvia: Singing and dance.
Man: That'll be <u>£60</u> then.
Sylvia: And what time do classes begin? I'm free all morning.
Man: The school opens at nine o'clock on Saturdays and classes start at <u>nine fifteen</u>.
Sylvia: Could I visit the school to see what it's like?
Man: Of course. We're in Marylebone High Street – that's <u>M-A-R-Y-L-E-B-O-N-E</u>.
Sylvia: Thanks. Can I get a bus rather than come by car?
Man: Yes, there's the 139 or the <u>189</u>. The 189 stops right outside the school.
Sylvia: That's great. When can I come and visit?
Man: Any time. What about next week?
Sylvia: OK, I'll do that. Thank you very much.
Man: Not at all. Goodbye.
Sylvia: Goodbye.

4 KET Reading Part 3

Ask the class to match sentences 1–4 with responses A–D. Play the recording again so they can check their answers.

Answers			
1 C	2 D	3 B	4 A

5 Students should work in pairs to do this exercise. Then play the recording so they can check their answers.

Answers				
1 G	**3** I	**5** F	**7** A	**9** C
2 E	**4** H	**6** J	**8** D	**10** B

Recording script

1

Girl: I can't come swimming tomorrow afternoon.
Boy: It doesn't matter.

2

Man: Ouch! You stood on my foot!
Woman: I'm so sorry!

3

Girl: Can I have a kilo of tomatoes, please?
Man: That'll be £1.50.

4

Girl: I've passed all my exams!
Boy: Congratulations!

5

Woman: Would you mind opening the window?
Man: Not at all.

6

Woman: Would you like a drink?
Man: Nothing for me, thanks.

7

Boy: Hi! How are you?
Girl: Fine, thanks.

8

Man: Hi! Is that Sally speaking?
Girl: No, it's Lisa.

9

Man: Can I sit here?
Woman: I'm afraid it's taken.

10

Boy: Let's go to the cinema.
Girl: Sorry, I can't. I'm busy.

E xtension activity

Each pair of students should have a copy of the *When do you say this?* game board on page 125 of the Teacher's Book and a dice. When they land on a square with a speech bubble, they should say when/where this phrase is said. If they land on a blank square they should wait for their next turn. The first person to the finish is the winner. If a student gets the answer wrong they miss a go.

Possible answers

3 When it's someone's birthday. Also *Many Happy Returns*!
6 You've won a prize, got married, passed an exam.
8 You've lost something, can't go to a party, etc.
9 On the phone, to say it's you speaking.
11 In a shop, when you don't want to buy something.
12 Something bad has happened. You've spilt something, lost something.
13 On the phone, to say who you are.
14 When someone has said *thank you* to you.
17 At meal times, to refuse more food.
18 When you meet someone for the first time. They say *How do you do?* and you say *How do you do?*
20 When someone looks unhappy.
21 When someone has a headache.
22 When something doesn't matter.
24 When someone is looking for you.
25 When you agree with someone.
26 When you didn't hear what someone said.
27 When you didn't hear what someone said, or you want to attract someone's attention or you want to pass them.
28 In a shop.
29 When you see someone you know, or you know they've been ill.

6 Check that the class understands *Across* and *Down*. The answers are to do with learning.

Answers

Across	*Down*
3 language	**1** pen
4 library	**2** study
6 board	**5** bookshelf
7 listen	**8** desk
9 teacher	**10** cupboard
11 history	**12** saw
13 homework	

G rammar extra

Explain that *rather than* is used when making a choice between two things.

7 Ask the class to write sentences that are true for them. They can do this in class or for homework.

Possible answers
2 I prefer to study maths rather than (study) English.
3 I prefer to read a book rather than watch TV.
4 I would like to learn Japanese rather than (learn) English.
5 I would prefer to play football rather than learn to sing.

6 I would like to play the guitar rather than (play) the piano.
7 I would prefer to be a teacher rather than (be) a doctor.
8 I would prefer to live in the USA rather than (live) in Australia.
9 I would like to marry someone rich rather than (marry) someone poor.
10 I would like to meet Brad Pitt rather than (meet) Jennifer Lopez.

Activity

Students should do this activity in small groups. At they end they need to make a presentation to the class.

Exam folder 8

Reading Part 3 Multiple choice

SB pages 90–91

Ask students to read the information about this part of the Reading and Writing paper. Refer them also to the Exam advice and the example from the answer sheet.

Answers				
11 C	13 A	15 A	17 A	19 C
12 B	14 B	16 D	18 H	20 F

 **The world of work**

15.1 Working hours	
Exam skills	Reading Part 4: Multiple choice
Grammar	Present perfect
Spelling	Words ending in -er and -or
Vocabulary	Jobs

15.2 Part-time jobs	
Grammar extra	*just* and *yet*
Exam skills	Listening Part 3: Multiple choice
Pronunciation	/ð/ and /θ/

Preparation

Make five photocopies of the *Good and bad points* grid on page 126 and write the name of a job in each of the five columns. This will be used in the Extension activity in 15.1. Make a copy of the recording script on page 127 for each student. This will be used in 15.2.

15.1 Working hours

SB pages 92–93

1

Answers
a nurse	c chef	e farmer
b receptionist	d journalist	

2 Ask students what verb form is used in the definitions (third person singular present simple). Remind them that most verbs in the third person singular need an *-s* ending, like these. The omission of *-s* is a common error at KET.

Answers
1 A nurse looks after those who are ill.
2 A farmer works outside in all kinds of weather.
3 A receptionist helps people on the phone.
4 A chef makes good things to eat.
5 A journalist finds out interesting information.

As a follow-up, ask students if they would like to do any of these jobs. Give them some time to think about their answers and then elicit ideas.

E xtension activity

Make five photocopies of the *Good and bad points* grid on page 126 and write the name of a job in each of the five rows. Divide the class into five groups and give each group one of the grids. Ask the groups to write down the positive and negative points about each job. Then ask each group to report their ideas to the class.

Reading

3 **KET Reading Part 4**

Tell students to use the colour coding to help them locate the answers to the questions in the text. Give them up to ten minutes to decide on their answers. Then go through the questions with them and explain any answers that they have found difficult.

Point out the use of possessive forms and apostrophes in question 5 (*Jamie's wife; a friend of Jamie's wife*).

Answers
1 B 2 C 3 A 4 B 5 C 6 C 7 A

Grammar

4 Concentrate on form rather than use here.

Answer
The present perfect is formed with *has/have* and the past participle.

5 Ask students to match the two uses of the present perfect (A and B) to the four examples (sentences 1–4). Then point out the common error with *ago* and ask students to decide on sentences 5–7.

Answers
1 B 2 A 3 A 4 B
You must use the past simple with *ago* because it refers to a completed action in definite past time.
5 A
6 incorrect
7 A

6 Ask students to work through the exercise and then compare answers. Elicit which sentences are incorrect and write the corrected tenses on the board, together with the time phrases (underlined below).

Answers
Sentences **3, 5** and **7** are incorrect:
3 The supermarket *advertised* for more staff <u>last week</u>.
5 Marion *became* a doctor <u>in 2002</u>.
7 Lee *arrived* for his meeting <u>an hour ago</u>.

7 Ask students to complete the text in pairs. Elicit answers and then ask students about the text. Would they like to live and go to school in another country? How would they feel if their parents travelled a long way every day for work, like Tom Stone?

Answers
  2 moved
  3 have made
  4 has travelled
  5 began
  6 decided
  7 meant / has meant
  8 wasn't
  9 found
  10 has taken

8 Ask students to quickly tick the things they have done and then elicit answers to the question *Have you ever been to London?* round the class. If someone says *Yes*, add a second question, for example *When was that? What did you do?* Then tell students to ask and answer in pairs, using the list and adding a suitable second question. Walk round and check which tenses they are using (present perfect for the first question, past simple for the second).

S pelling spot

9 Ask students to read the information before they do the exercise. This can be set as homework if necessary.

Answers
  1 photographer
  2 painter
  3 journalist
  4 actor
  5 doctor
The job in the yellow box is 'pilot'.

15.2 Part-time jobs
SB pages 94–95

1 Explain that in Britain many teenagers do newspaper delivery rounds, either before or after school. Elicit students' views on part-time evening or weekend jobs.

2 Ask students to read the advertisements and then elicit answers.

Answers
1 B   **2** A   **3** C

3 Elicit students' views on voluntary work (advertisement C).

G rammar extra

Ask students to read the information. The *Cambridge Learner Corpus* shows that accurate use of *just* at KET level is an indicator of above-average ability.

4 Ask students to write out the sentences in full. If time is short, ask students in pairs to write alternate sentences.

Answers
  1 The receptionist at the sports centre has just left a message for you.
  2 Tom hasn't met his new boss yet.
  3 They haven't sent me any information about the job yet.
  4 The newsagent has just stopped using paper boys and girls.
  5 My uncle has just given me a job in his café.
  6 Charlotte and Andy haven't found a photographer for their wedding yet.
  7 I have just chosen a computer course to go on.
  8 The supermarket manager hasn't paid Mike for his extra hours yet.

Listening

5 **KET Listening Part 3**

Give students exactly 20 seconds to read the questions and then play the recording twice.

Answers
1 B   **2** C   **3** B   **4** A   **5** B

Recording script

Sam: Melody Music Shop?

Kate: Yes, this is Kate Richards. How can I help?

Sam: My name's Sam Bennett. I've just seen your advertisement for a Saturday job. What are the hours?

Kate: The shop's open from ten to six but I need someone to <u>start at nine and stay until seven</u>. I'm always here from eight till eight on Saturdays so I really need help then!

Sam: I see. What kind of help?

Kate: Well, the most important thing is <u>helping customers, being a shop assistant</u>. I also want someone to do a bit of cleaning at the end of the day, so I can do the money.

Sam: Fine. How much do you pay?

Kate: If you aren't 18 yet, it's £ 5.25 an hour.

Sam: Actually, I am 18.

Kate: Then it's <u>£6.30</u>, and after nine months I'll pay £7.00 an hour.

Sam: Sounds great! Er … where is the shop? I've never been there!

Kate: It's not in the town centre. If you know <u>the university, it's about three minutes' walk from there</u>.

Sam: I live in Weston, but I can cycle along the river to get there.

Kate: That's true. Well, any other questions?

Sam: When can I come and see you about the job? I'm free on Wednesday afternoon.

Kate: Sorry, I've got a meeting then. How about Thursday or Friday?

Sam: <u>I can come early on Thursday</u>, at nine?

Kate: Fine. See you then.

Sam: Great!

P hotocopiable recording script activity ⋯⟶ page 127

Hand out copies of the recording script, where some words and phrases have been blanked out. Ask students to fill in as many as they can by looking again at the questions. Then play the recording, asking them to check their answers and add any missing words or phrases.

> **Answers**
> 1 hours   3 yet   5 free
> 2 most important thing   4 three minutes' walk

Pronunciation

6 The focus is on the sounds /ð/ as in *clothes* and /θ/ as in *thirsty*. Draw students' attention to the pictures. Play the recording and elicit the two sounds in the examples given: /ð/ and /θ/.

Ask students to repeat the words they hear and write them in group 1 or group 2. Play the recording twice if necessary.

> **Answers**
>
> | group 1 /ð/ | group 2 /θ/ |
> |---|---|
> | those | thunder |
> | leather | theatre |
> | than | thirty |
> | | month |
> | | nothing |

Recording script

thunder
than
those
theatre
thirty
month
leather
nothing

7 Explain that students should concentrate on the /ð/ sound (for example, *clothes*) the first time they listen and the /θ/ sound (for example, *thirsty*) the second time.

> **Answers**
> 1 I've worked for <u>the</u> last two mon(th)s in my fa(th)er's shop.
> 2 Let's look at all <u>these</u> job adverts toge(th)er.
> 3 I (th)ought you were working at <u>the</u> museum. Have you finished <u>there</u>?
> 4 Jenny, (th)anks for looking (th)rough my article.
> 5 <u>That</u> footballer earns a hundred and (th)irty (th)ousand euros a mon(th)!
> 6 My bro(th)er's just got a job in the nor(th) of Sweden.

Activity

Write these places on the board: *department store, hospital, hotel, film studio.* Ask students to brainstorm different jobs at each place. The group with the most jobs at the end wins. (Check that all the jobs are plausible for the place!)

> **Possible answers**
>
> | Place | department store |
> |---|---|
> | Jobs | manager, shop assistant, cleaner, driver |
>
> | Place | hospital |
> |---|---|
> | Jobs | doctor, nurse, ambulance driver, cleaner |
>
> | Place | hotel |
> |---|---|
> | Jobs | receptionist, cook, waiter, secretary, cleaner, engineer |
>
> | Place | film studio |
> |---|---|
> | Jobs | actor, cameraman, director, make-up person, (script)writer |

Writing folder 4

Writing Part 8 Information transfer

SB pages 96–97

Ask students to read the information about this part of the Reading and Writing paper. Explain that all the information that is needed in the answers appears on the question paper. In Part 8, candidates often lose marks unnecessarily by mis-copying a word or number.

1 Ask students to identify the kinds of text, which are typical of those used in KET Writing Part 8.

> **Answers**
> 1 ticket
> 2 poster
> 3 email

2 Ask students to find the information and then compare answers.

> **Answers**
> 1 07765 912448
> 2 *Animal Farm*
> 3 August 29 / 29.08
> 4 Juan Romero
> 5 £12.30
> 6 8.00 (pm) / 20.00
> 7 Brenton College (gardens)
> 8 £5.75

Part 8

Ask students to do the exam task, following the Exam advice given.

> **Answers**
> 51 lauratou@free.fr
> 52 18
> 53 23 June / June 23 / 23.06
> 54 Eastbourne
> 55 (£)60

16 Transport

16.1 Journeys	
Vocabulary	Transport (nouns and verbs)
Grammar	Modal verbs 2: *should,* *must/mustn't, need to / needn't,* *don't have to*

16.2 A day out	
Exam skills	Speaking Part 2 Listening Part 1: Multiple choice
Pronunciation	Weak and strong forms
Spelling	*i* or *e*?

16.1 Journeys

SB pages 98–99

1 Ask students to read the short texts (1–4) and decide in pairs whether they are true or false.

> **Answers**
> 1 False – The world's largest airport is King Khalid International Airport in Saudi Arabia, at 236 sq km (in 2004).
> 2 True
> 3 True
> 4 Partly false – It was a sheep, a duck and a chicken!

Vocabulary

2 Ask students to sort the transport words, writing the correct words alongside. Elicit answers.

> **Answers**
> 1 train   3 bicycle   5 plane   7 helicopter
> 2 coach   4 boat   6 taxi   8 horse

3 Ask students to match these words to their pictures and elicit any more words.

> **Answers**
> a 7   b 1   c 8   d 6   e 2   f 3   g 4   h 5

4 Elicit possible verb–noun collocations. Remind students to list new vocabulary like this where appropriate.

> **Answers**
> *catch* – a coach, a train, a plane
> *drive* – a train, a coach, a taxi
> *fly* – a plane, a helicopter
> *get* – a coach, a train, a plane, a helicopter, a boat, a taxi
> *get off/on* – a train, a coach, a bicycle, a boat, a plane, a helicopter, a horse
> *park* – a coach, a taxi
> *ride* – a bicycle, a horse
> *sail* – a boat

Grammar

5 Elicit the difference between examples 1 and 2, reminding students of the meaning of *must* if necessary. Then discuss the difference between sentences 3 and 4.

> **Answers**
> 1–2 *Should* gives advice here (and the girl doesn't have to act on it); *must* holds an obligation – it is essential that this girl is at Gate 43 by six o'clock or she won't be allowed to board the plane.
>
> 3–4 *Mustn't* is a prohibition (i.e. you must go earlier than six o'clock); *don't have to* means it isn't necessary to go there before six o'clock, but you can if you want to.

6 Suggest students complete the text on their own and then compare answers. Point out that they can use each verb once only.

> **Answers**
> 1 should
> 2 don't have to
> 3 must
> 4 mustn't

7 Ask students to decide in pairs which modal verbs are the closest in meaning to *need to* and *needn't* here. Explain that there is no *to* after *needn't* (*needn't to* is a common error at this level).

> **Answers**
> 1 *need to* – The closest verb is *must*.
> 2 *needn't* – The closest verb is *don't have to*.

8 Ask students to choose the correct modal verb in the sentences. If time is short, this exercise can be done for homework.

Answers
1 need to	**3** should	**5** mustn't
2 needn't	**4** need to	

9 Ask students to look at the example and describe the journey from London to Vizzavona. Elicit answers and then encourage students to describe another journey using as many transport words as they can. They could of course 'invent' a really complicated journey!

Possible answer
You need to fly to Paris first. You should change planes there and fly to Ajaccio. You needn't hire a car at the airport. You should take a taxi to the station. Then you can take a train to Vizzavona.

16.2 A day out

SB pages 100–101

Speaking

1 KET Speaking Part 2

Remind students that the Speaking test is in two parts. Ask them to decide whether the sentences are right or wrong in pairs. Elicit answers with reasons.

Answers
1 Right – Each candidate has a turn at asking the five questions.
2 Wrong – You must base your answers on the information given.
3 Right – You should talk only to the other candidate.
4 Wrong – You should use some other words and expressions, to make the conversation sound as natural as possible and show your language range.
5 Right!

2 Ask students to decide in pairs who will be Student A. Then ask students to turn to the relevant page and give them enough time to complete the task (about two minutes per turn).

E xtension activity

Offer to record each pair as they do a practice Speaking test, setting up individual times for this. Give them the recording so that they can note down their own errors, and suggest areas for improvement.

Listening

3 KET Listening Part 1

Explain that students will hear each conversation twice. Play the recording and then elicit answers.

Answers
1 B **2** C **3** C **4** B **5** A

Recording script

1 Which train is leaving next?

Man: Excuse me, is this the Bristol train?
Woman: No, this one's leaving for Oxford in five minutes. There's been a change to the Bristol train. You need to go over the bridge to platform 4.
Man: Oh dear, have I got enough time to get there?
Woman: Plenty, <u>that's the London train that's ready to leave</u>. Yours will be the next train after that one.

Now listen again.
(The recording is repeated.)

2 How will the girl get to the cinema?

Girl: Can you tell me where the ABC cinema is, please?
Man: Certainly. Turn <u>left at the next traffic lights and then take the second on the right</u>.
Girl: Is that Green Street?
Man: That's the turning after. It's Robertson Road you need. Go nearly to the end and you'll see the cinema on your left.

Now listen again.
(The recording is repeated.)

3 Where is Kate's boat now?

Adam: Hi, Kate! We've just crossed over to the island now. How far have you got?
Kate: Well, Adam, I can't describe anything because <u>there's water all around</u>. We went under a bridge about a quarter of an hour ago, if that means anything?
Adam: Sounds like you'll reach us in about an hour then.
Kate: Sorry it's taking so long. Bye.

Now listen again.
(The recording is repeated.)

4 How will the woman get to work today?

Anne: Mike, it's Anne. Listen, there are no trains this morning because of last night's winds. <u>Is it OK if I get a taxi</u> in to work? Will the company pay?
Mike: Can't you use your car? It's much cheaper.
Anne: I'm afraid it's at the garage.
Mike: <u>OK, then</u>, but make sure you ask for a receipt. See you later.

Now listen again.
(The recording is repeated.)

5 Where is the nearest petrol station?

Woman: Can you tell me where I can get some petrol?

Man: Well, the cheapest place is on the motorway. It's not far. You can get on at the next roundabout.

Woman: I really need a nearer one. I haven't got much left.

Man: I see. Turn left by the lights, then, and you'll find one on the right <u>next to a bank</u>, about 200 metres down that road.

Now listen again.

(The recording is repeated.)

Pronunciation

4 Ask students to listen carefully to the examples. If necessary, play the recording again so that students recognise the weak forms. Then ask them to decide about sentences 1–8, writing W or S. Check answers, playing the recording again and pausing so that they can hear each one.

Answers						
2 W	3 S	4 W	5 W	6 W	7 S	8 W

S pelling spot

5 These examples of errors are taken from the *Cambridge Learner Corpus*.

Answers
1 museum
2 airport
3 hospital
4 (correct)
5 university

Activity

Ask students to take it in turns to give directions.
Walk round listening as they do the activity and summarise any recurring errors on the board afterwards.

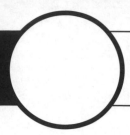

Units 13–16 Revision

SB pages 102–106

This revision unit recycles the language and topics from Units 13–16, as well as providing exam practice for Reading Part 5 and Writing Part 7.

Speaking

1 Ask students to draft their questions and then ask and answer in pairs.

Possible questions
2 Shall we go swimming at the beach later?
3 Do you want to go for a pizza after class?
4 What does your favourite jacket look like?
5 What's the weather going to be like at the weekend?
6 How much does it cost to get in to the club?
7 Have you visited any other countries?
8 Have you read any good books recently?

Grammar

2

Answers
The correct sentences are:
1 B   **2** A   **3** C   **4** B

3

Answers
1 C   **2** B   **3** B   **4** A   **5** C   **6** B   **7** A   **8** C

Vocabulary

4 Ask students to do this in pairs.

Answers
Jobs
Nouns: artist, chef, dentist, farmer, journalist, paint, photographer, secretary, waiter
Verbs: fix, grow, paint, phone, write

Weather
Nouns: cloud, fog, rain, snow, thunderstorm, wind
Verbs: rain, snow

Transport
Nouns: boat, car, helicopter, plane, taxi
Verbs: catch, drive, fly, get off, sail, take off

5

Answers
1 C   **2** B   **3** B   **4** A   **5** A   **6** C   **7** B   **8** C

Writing

6

Answers
1 any
2 one/magazine
3 ago
4 lots/plenty
5 every/each/this/next
6 most
7 something
8 by
9 were
10 never

Reading Part 3

Questions 1–5

Complete the five conversations.

For questions **1–5**, mark **A**, **B** or **C**.

Example:

0

Is this seat taken?

A I'm not on it.

B Not at the moment.

C No, nobody.

Answer: **0**

---

1 What do you do?
    A I studied.
    B I'm a teacher.
    C I'm very busy.

2 What's the weather like?
    A Very fine.
    B It's too nice.
    C Not bad.

3 How long have you studied English?
    A For four years.
    B Four years ago.
    C In four years.

4 You don't have to leave now.
    A Why not?
    B Why haven't I?
    C Why don't you?

5 How much does the bus cost?
    A Not at all.
    B It's free.
    C You must pay now.

© Cambridge University Press, 2005

Questions 6–10

Complete the conversation.
What does Alana say to Nico?

For questions **6–10**, mark the correct letter **A–H**.

Example:

Nico: What are you going to do in the school holidays, Alana?

Alana: 0 ....   Answer: 0 [A B C D E F G [H filled]]

Nico: That sounds interesting. Where are
            you going?

Alana: 6 ....

Nico: I'd really like to do that.
            Is it expensive?

Alana: 7 ....

Nico: Great! So, are you taking a tent?

Alana: 8 ....

Nico: I've got to work washing the
            dishes in my father's restaurant
            in July.

Alana: 9 ....

Nico: Not really. He says I need to
            study more, so I'm going to a
            language school in England.

Alana: 10 ....

Nico: That's what my dad says. I think
            it'll be too cold and rainy to do
            anything but study!

A I'd really like to do that. You
     know it'll really help you with
     your English exam.

B We're getting a train to Brindisi
     and then a boat to Greece.

C Yes, I like it very much.

D That's a pity. But will he give
     you some free time in August?

E Not as much as a plane ticket!

F Rome – then we went to Sicily.

G I like to be comfortable so we
     won't camp. What about you?

H I'm going to go travelling with
     some friends.

Writing Part 8

Read the email to Luke and the poster about boat trips.

Complete Luke's notes.

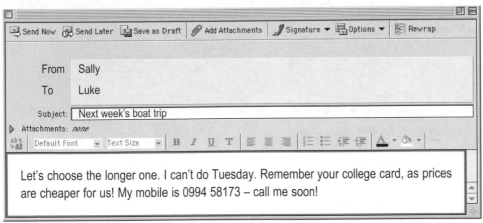

From   Sally
To   Luke
Subject: Next week's boat trip
Attachments: *none*

Let's choose the longer one. I can't do Tuesday. Remember your college card, as prices are cheaper for us! My mobile is 0994 58173 – call me soon!

RIVER TRIPS

Tuesdays and Thursdays

Boats leave Duxford Bridge at 1.30 pm
(4-hour journey to Castletown)

OR Henleaze Bridge at 3 pm
(90-minute journey to Melton)

Tickets
Castletown: £12.50 (£8.80 students)
Melton: £9.00 (£6.20 students)

Phone 0145 669270

LUKE'S NOTES	
Number of tickets	*2*
Boat trip to	**1**
Day	**2**
Price per ticket	**3** £
Place to get boat	**4**
Sally's phone number	**5**

© Cambridge University Press, 2005

Listening Part 2

Listen to Harry telling Joanna what jobs people in his family do.
Which job does each person do?

For questions **1–5**, write a letter **A–H** next to each person.

You will hear the conversation twice.

Example:

0 Harry's father | B |

People		**Jobs**
1 Harry's mother	☐	**A** artist
2 James	☐	**B** chef
3 Uncle Bill	☐	**C** doctor
4 Aunt Anne	☐	**D** journalist
5 Diane	☐	**E** nurse
		F photographer
		G pilot
		H teacher

© Cambridge University Press, 2005

Test 4 Key

Reading Part 3

Answers

1 B	3 A	5 B	7 E	9 D
2 C	4 A	6 B	8 G	10 A

Writing Part 8

Answers
1 Castletown
2 Thursday
3 (£)8.80
4 Duxford Bridge
5 0994 58173

Listening Part 2

Answers

1 E   2 H   3 F   4 C   5 G

Recording script

Listening Part 2

Listen to Harry telling Joanna what jobs people in his family do. Which job does each person do? For questions 1 to 5, write a letter, A to H, next to each person. You will hear the conversation twice.

Harry: Hi, Joanna.

Joanna: Oh, hi Harry.

Harry: Good news! My dad's just got a new job.

Joanna: Really!

Harry: Yes, he's become head chef at the new restaurant in town.

Joanna: Great. Do you think your mum'll stop working at the hospital now?

Harry: No, she loves being a nurse there. I think she's going to do fewer hours, so she can go to more art classes in her free time.

Joanna: And is your brother James still teaching?

Harry: He is, but he'd like to become a journalist one day.

Joanna: Can your uncle find him a job on his newspaper?

Harry: I don't think so. Uncle Bill doesn't work in the newspaper office because he's out all day taking pictures for them.

Joanna: I see. What does his wife do?

Harry: Aunt Anne's a doctor. She works very long hours, just like chefs do! Her daughter Diane works hard too, but she really loves her job.

Joanna: Is she an artist?

Harry: That's her husband. Diane flies planes for one of the airlines.

Joanna: Isn't she lucky, travelling to different places!

Harry: Yes, very.

Now listen again.

(The recording is repeated.)

 **Science and technology**

17.1 Techno Star	
Reading	Quiz
Grammar	Infinitive of purpose
Exam skills	Reading Part 5: Multiple-choice cloze

17.2 Science is great!	
Exam skills	Listening Part 3: Multiple choice
Pronunciation	Contractions
Vocabulary	Collocations with *get*, *make*, *watch* and *see*
Spelling	Correcting mistakes
Grammar extra	The infinitive – with and without *to*

Preparation

Make a copy of the recording script on page 128 for each student. This will be used in 17.2.

17.1 Techno Star

SB pages 104–105

Reading

1 Ask students to do the quiz to find out what their attitude to science and technology is. When they have finished ask them to compare answers with a partner. Do they agree with their results?

Grammar

2 Ask students to look back through the quiz and underline all the infinitives with *to*. Explain that these are infinitives of purpose which are used when saying why we do something. For more practice, refer students to the Grammar folder on page 144 of the Student's Book.

Answers
1 You use a computer *to talk* to people in chat rooms.
2 You switch on *to check* your email about once a week.
3 You use a computer *to do* your homework.
4 You'd like a robot *to help* clean your room.

3 This exercise gives more practice in the use of infinitives of purpose. Check the vocabulary is familiar and then ask students to work through it.

Answers
2 to tell	4 to call	6 to listen	8 to buy
3 to turn on	5 to keep	7 to study	

4 Ask students to work through this exercise in pairs. They should think of as many reasons as possible why people do these things.

Possible answers
2 People listen to the radio to hear the latest music and news.
3 People have parties to have fun and to celebrate a birthday.
4 People go to other countries to learn a language and to find out about different cultures.
5 People play football to keep fit and to have fun.
6 People use a laptop computer to work outside or to work on the train.
7 People read magazines to find out about one of their interests.
8 People take photos to remember a person or place.
9 People learn English to get a good job or to travel.

5 Take a few minutes to have a class discussion about computer games.

6 **KET Reading Part 5**

The text is about the man who worked for Nintendo and invented the Game Boy. Set students a few questions to answer on the first reading, for example:
When was Nintendo started? (1889)
What was Gunpei's new game first called? (*Ultrahand*)
When was the first Game Boy made? (1989)

It is important students really understand the text before they start to do the exam task. It is a very bad idea to go straight to the multiple-choice questions without reading the text first.

Answers
1 C   2 B   3 C   4 A   5 C   6 C   7 A   8 C

17.2 Science is great!

SB pages 106–107

1 The listening task in exercise 2 is about a James Bond exhibition in London. Ask the class to brainstorm what they know about James Bond. Elicit the word *gadgets* so they understand what these are.

Listening

2 **KET Listening Part 3**

Play the recording twice.

Answers
1 C   2 A   3 B   4 C   5 C

Recording script

Boy: Hi, Vanessa! Did you have a good weekend?

Vanessa: Great! I went to see a special James Bond exhibition at the Science Museum.

Boy: Sounds interesting, but I think museums are too expensive – I paid £8 last time I went.

Vanessa: This was only £6.50. I did buy a guidebook as well – that was an extra £2.95.

Boy: How did you get there?

Vanessa: You can take the underground, but I went by bus. It stops just outside. I got very tired walking around the museum though.

Boy: What did you see?

Vanessa: James Bond's helicopter, which was my favourite, and the tiny camera, and his car, things like that.

Boy: It sounds great! How early can you go in? At nine?

Vanessa: Not until ten, and we didn't get there until eleven thirty, so there wasn't enough time to see everything.

Boy: Can you eat there?

Vanessa: Yes. You can even take a picnic! I had a sandwich at a café but you can get a hot meal at the restaurant.

Boy: I'd really like to go. I'm free next Saturday – that's 23rd April.

Vanessa: The exhibition's on until the 27th, so the Saturday may be busy.

Boy: Well, I'll go on the 24th then.

Photocopiable recording script activity ···⟩ page 128

Photocopy the recording script and play the recording again. Ask students to locate the answers and make them aware of the distractors.

Pronunciation

3

Answers
1 There was not enough time to see everything.
2 I would really like to go.
3 I am free next Saturday – that is 23rd April.
4 The exhibition is on until the 27th.

4 Students should work through this exercise, forming contractions. There are two sentences where contractions can't be formed. Play the recording so students can check their answers.

Answers
1 I'm   3 Who's   5 –
2 Aren't you   4 I'd   6 Dan's
7 They can't, it's (It would probably be clearer for the meaning of the sentence if 'it has closed' is not contracted.)
8 –

Vocabulary

5 Collocations were introduced in Unit 5. This unit covers *get*, *make*, *watch* and *see*.

Answers
get – a job (*Get a TV*, in the sense of *buy a TV* is also a possibility, though this is not really a collocation.)
make – a noise, a film, friends
watch – TV, a film
see – a film, friends

We normally say *watch TV* and *see a film*, though *watch a film* is sometimes also possible.

6

Answers
1 make   3 make   5 see
2 get   4 watch   6 seen

S pelling spot

7 This can be done in class or at home. It contains typical errors made by KET candidates.

Answers

Dear Carl,

I want to sell a mobile because my girlfriend bought me a new one last weekend. It is two years old and the price is about $100. My telephone number is 956531.

Regards,
Phil

E xtension activity

For homework ask students to write a For Sale notice for a computer game, CD player or computer that they own. They should include details of:
- how much it originally cost
- the sale price
- details of the product.

G rammar extra

Explain the use of the infinitive with and without *to*. It may be useful at this point to revise the *-ing* form of verbs, which was covered in Unit 11, as students sometimes wrongly use an *-ing* form instead of the infinitive.

8 Students can work through this exercise in pairs or individually. These are typical KET candidate errors.

Answers
1 I'd like *to see* you next weekend.
2 I must *arrive* home at 10.00.
3 I would like *to sell* my books.
4 I want *to buy* it.
5 You can *go* to a museum there.
6 I have decided *to study* chemistry.
7 She should *visit* London.
8 I hope *to see* you soon.
9 We need *to do* our homework tonight.
10 We went to London *to see* the London Eye.

Activity

This activity recycles vocabulary learnt in Unit 10 – materials. Ask the class to guess what the object described is. (Answer – a mobile phone.)

Ask them, either in class or for homework, to write a short description of an everyday object. The rest of the class must guess what it is.

Exam folder 9

Listening Part 3   Multiple choice

SB pages 108–109

Ask students to read the information about this part of the Listening paper. Also make sure they fully understand the Exam advice.

Before the exam task, go through the two examples of exam-type questions and make students aware of the use of distractors in the exam. They should realise that they will often hear more than one of the three options mentioned on the recording and that they have to process the information to get the right answer.

Answers
11 B   12 A   13 C   14 C   15 A

Recording script

Listen to Ellie talking to Chris about Lynne, his sister. For questions 11 to 15, tick A, B, or C. You will hear the conversation twice. Look at questions 11 to 15 now. You have 20 seconds.

Ellie: Hi, Chris. I hear Lynne's here. I thought she was coming on Saturday.

Chris: Yeah, well, she came on Wednesday because she has to be at work again on Monday.

Ellie: That's a pity. How is Lynne's new job with that computer company?

Chris: Great. She did a course in London and now she's in New York for a year. Next year she may go to Hong Kong!

Ellie: That's brilliant! I'd like to work with computers.

Chris: Me too, but Lynne didn't study anything to do with computers at school. Dad taught her at home and then she did maths at university.

Ellie: She must work hard.

Chris: Yes, but she gets four weeks holiday a year. Next year it'll be six – my dad only gets five!

Ellie: Can I see her tomorrow?

Chris: Of course. Come in the afternoon. She'll be in bed all morning.

Ellie: OK, I'll come after lunch. I've bought her a watch for her birthday.

Chris: She really wanted me to get her a camera but I only had enough money for a computer game, so I got that!

Ellie: I'm sure she'll like it. See you tomorrow.

Now listen again.
(The recording is repeated.)

18 Health and well-being

18.1 Keeping well!

Vocabulary	Parts of the body
Exam skills	Reading Part 6: Spelling
	Reading Part 3: Functional English
	Listening Part 5: Note taking
Grammar extra	Word order of time phrases
Pronunciation	Linking sounds

18.2 A long and happy life

Exam skills	Reading Part 4: Right, Wrong, Doesn't say
	Writing Part 9: Writing a note
Grammar	First conditional
Spelling	Words which don't double their last letter, as in *helped, needed*

Preparation

Make one copy of the *How stressed are you?* board game on page 129 for each group of four students. This will be used in the Extension activity in 18.2. Each group will also need a dice.

18.1 Keeping well!

SB pages 110–111

Vocabulary

1 Ask the class to correctly spell the parts of the body 1–12 and then to match them with the pictures.

Answers

1 head d	5 hands j	9 ear c
2 hair b	6 back l	10 mouth i
3 neck k	7 leg a	11 nose e
4 arm f	8 foot h	12 eye g

2 **KET Reading Part 6**

The task is about words connected with health. Students must decide what the word is and spell it correctly.

Answers

2 nurse	4 medicine	6 chemist
3 ambulance	5 temperature	

Extension activity

Ask students to do the same as the above by writing six definitions of other words to do with health, the body and fitness. They must then get their partner to guess the words.

3 **KET Reading Part 3**

The section deals with responses to common medical complaints. Students should work in pairs to match the complaint to the response. There may be more than one appropriate response depending on nationality.

Suggested answers

1 H	3 E	5 C	7 G	9 I
2 J	4 B	6 F	8 A	10 D

4 Ask students to work in pairs and look at the pictures. They should take it in turns to say what is wrong with them and to give advice.

Possible answers

1 I think I've broken my leg.
 – Why don't you go to Casualty?
2 I've got stomach ache.
 – Why don't you take a painkiller?
3 I've got toothache.
 – You need to see a dentist.
4 I've cut my knee.
 – You should put a plaster on it.
5 I've got a cold.
 – You need to drink some hot lemon juice and go to bed.
6 I've got a headache.
 – Why don't you take an aspirin?

Listening

5 **KET Listening Part 5**

Tell the class that they are going to hear a recorded message giving information about chemists which are open in the local area. Ask them to read through the questions and then play the recording.

Answers

1 6.30 (pm)
2 Peters
3 17
4 (the) cinema
5 0921 6582

Recording script

Thank you for calling for information about the opening hours for chemists in your area. This information is for the week of the 15th to the 21st December. There are two chemists, one in Sandford and one in Dursley. Bridges Chemist in Sandford opens at eight forty-five from Monday to Saturday and closes at <u>six thirty pm</u> Monday to Friday and at twelve thirty pm on Saturday. The shop is at 53 Green Street, Sandford. There is a small car park next to the shop.

Outside those hours, please go to Peters. That's <u>P-E-T-E-R-S.</u> This is in Dursley at number <u>17</u> The High Street. It's on the other side of the road to <u>the cinema</u> and is open from ten thirty am to four thirty pm on Sundays and has late opening to eight pm on weekdays. The telephone number is <u>0921 6582</u>. Ring this number if you need to talk to the chemist at night. You can park in The High Street on Sundays.

Grammar extra

Refer the class to the information in their books.

6 Students should work through the exercise. It is more usual to place the time phrase at the end of the sentence, although it depends on which part of the sentence you wish to emphasise – the time or the action. Where it is possible to place it at the beginning of the sentence, this is shown in brackets.

> **Answers**
> 1 (Last night) I was at a big party last night.
> 2 (On Saturday) I'll come shopping on Saturday.
> 3 We have been to the beach every day.
> 4 (After work) I went to the chemist's after work.
> 5 They usually sleep well at night.
> 6 (Today) I bought some new trainers today.

Pronunciation

7

> **Answers**
> 1 Can you call an ambulance?
> 2 Fruit and vegetables are very good for you.
> 3 You should do some exercise every day.
> 4 Watching TV all weekend is not good for you.
> 5 Make sure you get enough sleep every night.

18.2 A long and happy life
SB pages 112–113

1 Ask a few general questions to introduce the topic of sleep.

Reading

2 `KET Reading Part 4`

Ask the class to read the article quickly to find out who is the oldest person mentioned (Shirali Muslimov).

Students should then read the article again and answer the questions.

> **Answers**
> 1 A   2 B   3 C   4 B   5 C   6 A   7 A   8 A

Grammar

Ask the class to find the sentence in the text which begins with *If* …

> **Answers**
> If you eat a little but often, you will live a long life.
>
> The tenses used are:
> *If* + *eat* (present simple), + *will live* (future simple)

3

> **Suggested answers**
> 1 E   2 D   3 A   4 F   5 B   6 C

For more practice, refer students to the Grammar folder on page 145 of the Student's Book.

Extension activity

Photocopy the *How stressed are you?* board game on page 129 and give one copy to each group of four students. They will need a dice to play. The questions should not be taken too seriously.

4 The class can work in groups or pairs to do this discussion on health. Ask them to talk about the ideas mentioned and to add two ideas of their own.

5 Ask students to work in pairs and discuss the type of problems they may have on a camping holiday, and how they will solve them.

6 The class should write down four sentences which are true for them. They should all begin with *If*.

7 KET Writing Part 9

This can be done in class or set for homework.

Sample answer
Dear Tim,

I want to get fit so I can climb a mountain with my father in the summer. I am going to go running every day and I will do this from tomorrow morning!

Love,
Jules

This answer includes all the key points and is error-free. It would receive full marks.

S pelling spot

8 Check students understand the explanation and ask them to complete the exercise.

Answers
1 ✓
2 ✗ – faster
3 ✓
4 ✗ – stopping
5 ✓
6 ✓
7 ✗ – thinner
8 ✗ – swimming

Activity

Students should stand up and wander around the class to do this activity. They should ask four classmates about their dreams and sleeping habits and report back to the class.

Exam folder 10

Reading Part 4 Multiple choice
SB pages 114–115

Ask students to read the information about this part of the Reading and Writing paper. Refer them also to the Exam advice. Go through the example with them and explain that there are distractors in the text. It is helpful if students underline the part of the text which contains the answer.

Answers
21 B   22 C   23 B   24 A   25 C   26 A   27 B

Language and communication

19.1 Let's communicate!	
Vocabulary	Communicating
Exam skills	Listening Part 2: Multiple matching Writing part 7: Open cloze
Pronunciation	Stressed syllables
Grammar extra	Prepositions of place
Spelling	The sound /i:/

19.2 Different languages	
Exam skills	Reading Part 5: Multiple-choice cloze
Grammar	Prepositions of time
Vocabulary	Countries, languages, nationalities

Preparation
Make a copy of the recording script on page 130 for each student. This will be used in 19.1

19.1 Let's communicate!

SB pages 116–117

Vocabulary

1 Suggest students spend a couple of minutes finding the words on their own and then compare the words in pairs. Elicit answers and check understanding if necessary, using the pictures.

Answers	
envelope	fax
text	email
message	receive
chat	call
send	mobile
telephone	postcard
write	ring
note	internet
letter	

a	l	i	o	r	o	m	a	y	i
w	e	n	v	e	l	o	p	e	n
r	t	f	o	c	c	b	o	s	t
i	t	a	f	e	a	i	s	r	e
t	e	x	t	i	l	l	t	i	r
e	r	n	e	v	l	e	c	n	n
n	w	e	m	e	s	s	a	g	e
o	c	h	a	t	o	m	r	i	t
t	o	r	i	s	e	n	d	a	l
e	t	e	l	e	p	h	o	n	e

2 Ask students to discuss in pairs for about five minutes. Then elicit ideas.

Listening

3 **KET Listening Part 2**

Remind students that in this matching task the example letter (B) cannot be used again, so there are seven choices for five questions. Play the recording twice before eliciting answers.

Answers				
1 D	**2** F	**3** A	**4** E	**5** G

Recording script

Paul: Hello, Ruth.

Ruth: Hi, Paul. I got your fax at work this morning. Congratulations on the new job!

Paul: Thanks. I didn't have your email address with me, or <u>Mario's</u>, so I spoke to him on his <u>mobile</u> just now.

Ruth: Have you told <u>Anna</u> yet?

Paul: Well, I left a message on her <u>answerphone</u>, but I think she's away. If I don't hear from her, I'll send her a text tomorrow.

Ruth: And what about your brother, <u>Jack</u>? He's away too, isn't he?

Paul: Yes, in Argentina. I <u>emailed</u> him from home this morning after I opened the letter about the job. I know he'll be pleased.

Ruth: Was <u>Tessa</u> still in the flat when the post arrived?

Paul: No, but I've left a <u>big note</u> on the kitchen table for her.

Ruth: Remember to phone <u>your professor</u> and tell him.

Paul: I can't because the number at his university has changed.

Ruth: Oh, and he's no longer on email, is he?

Paul: It doesn't matter. I've already told him the news on a <u>postcard</u>. I bought one of that Moroccan carpet we saw at the museum.

Ruth: He'll like that.

P hotocopiable recording script activity ···⟩ page 130

Make copies of the recording script on page 130. Several verbs in verb–noun collocations are blanked out. Ask students to add each verb in the correct tense, using the nouns to help them remember the verb. Then play the recording again to check their answers.

Answers			
1 got	3 left	5 opened	7 changed
2 spoke	4 send	6 arrived	8 told

Pronunciation

4 Ask students to place a star or dot above the stressed syllable of each word. Play the recording twice and check answers the second time, pausing the recording after each sentence.

Suggest students mark the stress on new words they write down, particularly when they are of three or more syllables.

Answers

1 Con|gra|tu|la|tions on the new job!

2 I didn't have your e|mail address.

3 I left a mess|age on her an|swer|phone.

4 Yes, in Ar|gen|ti|na.

5 Re|mem|ber to phone your pro|fess|or and tell him.

6 The num|ber at his u|ni|ver|si|ty has changed.

7 I bought one of that Mo|rocc|an car|pet we saw at the mu|se|um.

Grammar

Explain that KET candidates often make mistakes with prepositions. This lesson focuses on prepositions of place and 19.2 looks at prepositions of time.

5 Give students two minutes to do the exercise and then elicit answers, writing some of their examples on the board.

Answers		
2 on	4 in / on	6 in
3 in	5 at	7 at

6 Ask students to correct the sentences in pairs. Elicit answers.

Answers

1 You can call me *on* my cell phone: 22 59 67 81.

2 I'll meet you *at/in* the supermarket in West Street.

3 I'm *on* holiday now in Istanbul.

4 You can stay *in/at* my house.

5 The hotel is *in* the centre of the town.

6 We live *in* a new house in Magka.

7 (correct)

8 If you are interested, find me *in* room 12.

7 KET Writing Part 7

This exam-level task can be set for homework if time is short.

Answers

1 many

2 because/as/since

3 some

4 on

5 In

6 these

7 Which

8 will

9 me

10 everyone/everybody

S pelling spot

8 Ask students to study the examples and add the missing vowels. Dictionaries can be used to check spellings if necessary.

Answers		
1 received	3 speak	5 week
2 free; each	4 field	6 kilo

E xtension activity

Organise the class into groups of three or six. Explain that you are going to have a competition to produce as many words with the same spelling as possible. Write the three words *see*, *mean*, and *believe* on the board and underline their /iː/ spellings, as in the Spelling spot lists.
Give students up to ten minutes to write down more words with the same spelling (in beginning, middle or end positions). They could take one spelling each (group of three) or per pair (group of six), and then add to each others' lists. If students are struggling to think of words, suggest they look through the Vocabulary folder on pages 147–150, or give them one dictionary per group. Note that the *-ie-* spelling is less frequent than the other two, so students may not come up with as many words. The group with the highest number of correct spellings wins.

Possible answers
1 seen, been, feet, bee, sleep, green, referee, free, cheese, tree, week
2 read, ice cream, tea, eat, dream, pleased, cheap, jeans, clean, team, teacher, colleague, easy, speak, speaker, each, beach, peace, reach
3 believed, field, niece, piece, achieve, brief, chief, thief

19.2 Different languages

SB pages 118–119

1 Elicit answers from students and talk about your own use of dialects or other languages.

2 Decide as a class whether there are more or fewer dialects than 20 years ago and discuss why. Possible reasons for less use of dialects include better communications, people travelling more, television, the internet. Any growth in dialect use can be explained by a greater sense of regionalism (some dialects are now being taught in schools) and the rediscovery of local traditions.

Reading

3 **KET Reading Part 5**

Ask students to read the article and then decide on the answers.

Answers
1 C   2 B   3 C   4 B   5 A   6 C   7 B   8 C

Grammar

4 Ask students to complete the explanation with the correct prepositions.

Answers
We use *in* with years, etc.
We use *on* with days, etc.
We use *at* with times, etc.

5 Ask students to work in pairs and get Student Bs to put up their hands. They should turn to page 133 and answer Student As' questions about Lara's timetable. Student As should fill in the timetable and, when they have finished, check it against the one on page 133.

6 Suggest students fill in the chart in pairs.

Answers

country	nationality	language(s) spoken
Argentina	Argentinian	Spanish
Brazil	Brazilian	Portuguese
Chile	Chilean	Spanish
France	French	French
Greece	Greek	Greek
Italy	Italian	Italian
Mexico	Mexican	Spanish
Morocco	Moroccan	Arabic, French
Switzerland	Swiss	French, German, Italian, Romansch

Activity

Divide the class into two teams and ask students in each team to number themselves from 15 onwards (this gives practice of the larger numbers). Say the numbers and ask students to put up their hands as their number is called. There should be two students with the same number, one on each team. If one team has an extra person, take that person's number yourself for the other team.

Call a number, for example 22. The person whose number it is in team A should say the name of a country. The team B person then has to name one language that is spoken there. The next time, the team B person says the name of a country and the team A person has to name a language. Keep alternating in this way.

Keep a record of points awarded on the board, in tally style (‖‖‖ = 5) and add up the points at the end to decide the winning team.

Here is a longer list of countries and languages, in case students need more help.

country	nationality	language(s) spoken
Algeria	Algerian	Arabic, French
Austria	Austrian	German
Belgium	Belgian	Flemish, French
China	Chinese	Chinese
Croatia	Croat	Croatian
Denmark	Danish	Danish
Egypt	Egyptian	Arabic
Eire (Ireland)	Irish	English, Irish, Gaelic
Finland	Finn	Finnish
Germany	German	German
Holland	Dutch	Dutch
Japan	Japanese	Japanese
Korea	Korean	Korean
Norway	Norwegian	Norwegian
Poland	Polish	Polish
Portugal	Portuguese	Portuguese
Russia	Russian	Russian
Slovenia	Slovenian	Slovene
Spain	Spanish	Spanish
Sweden	Swedish	Swedish
Turkey	Turkish	Turkish

Writing folder 5

Writing Part 9   Short message

SB pages 120–121

Ask students to read the information about this part of the Reading and Writing paper. There are two kinds of Part 9 task: 'with input' and 'instructions only'. Writing folder 3 covered the 'with input' type.

1 These KET answers have been taken from the *Cambridge Learner Corpus*. Ask students to decide on the three points in the task, choosing from A–E.

> **Answers**
> A, C, D

2 Elicit views, asking students for their reasons why.

> **Answers** (and marking information)
> Answer 3 is the best and would score 5 marks. It has only one error (*in the bus stop*) and all parts of the message are clearly communicated.
> Answer 2 is the worst and would score 1 mark. Only one piece of information is communicated and the answer is short (23 words).
> Answer 1 would score 4 marks. It is just long enough at 25 words and contains some errors in spelling and grammar.
> Answer 4 would score 3 marks. All three parts of the message are attempted but the reader needs to interpret some of the information. There are also some errors in grammar and spelling. Although there is no penalty at KET for answers that are longer than 35 words, this message reads unclearly at 53 words. See improved version in 4 below.

3 Suggest students do this on their own and then compare answers.

> **Corrected answers**
>
> **1**
> Dear Pat
> I'll be free at 10 a.m. We can meet ~~us~~ at Paul's ~~caffe~~. I'd like to buy a skirt. See you on Saturday.
> Love Anya
>
> **2**
> Dear Pat: <u>I will go</u> for two hours. <u>I will meet with</u> John and I <u>will want to buy</u> a red bicycle.
> Your friend
>
> **3**
> Dear Pat I think it is a great idea to go shopping together. We could meet *at* the bus stop at 12 o'clock in the morning. I'd like to buy some pens.
> See you soon. Claudia
>
> **4**
> Yes, <u>I am coming</u> with you <u>to shopping</u> on Saturday. I'll probably be free <u>at the lunch</u>. We'll meet <u>us</u> *at* the shopping centre in town. I want to buy <u>me</u> <u>two trousers</u> and a top. Perhaps, I <u>want to buy also</u> a <u>robe</u>. And you, what do you want to buy? From your best friend
> Sylvie

4 Explain why it is better for students to write according to the word limits given (see marking information in 2 above).

> **Improved answer**
> Dear Pat,
>
> I'm free to go shopping at lunchtime on Saturday. Let's meet at the shopping centre in town. I want to buy two pairs of trousers, a top and perhaps a dress too.
> From your best friend,
> Sylvie

5 Ask students to write their answers following the advice given.

> **Sample answer**
> Hi Jan,
>
> Let's meet at the cinema at 7.30 tomorrow. I really want to see Lost in Translation. You'll love it because your favourite actor, Bill Murray, is in it. See you inside.
>
> Love,
> Kirsten
> (35 words)

20 People

20.1	Famous people
Grammar	Review of tenses
Exam skills	Reading Part 4: Multiple choice

20.2	**Lucky people**
Exam skills	Listening Part 4: Note taking
	Speaking Part 2
	Writing Part 6: Vocabulary
	Reading Part 2: Multiple choice
Pronunciation	Sentence stress
Vocabulary	Describing people
Spelling	*ck* or *k*?

Preparation

For the activity in 20.2, photocopy the KET 'money' on pages 131–132 of the Teacher's Book and cut it into notes. You will need about 30 × 1000 KETO notes and 20 × 2000 notes. Add more 1000 notes for a large class.

20.1 Famous people

SB pages 122–123

1 Elicit who is shown in which picture: top left Arnold Schwarzenegger, top right David Beckham, bottom Kelly Osbourne. Lead a class discussion on the questions raised.

2 Elicit answers round the class.

3 Suggest students answer the questions in pairs.

> **Answers**
> 1 A   2 C   3 B   4 C   5 B

Grammar

4 Ask students to do the exercise in pairs. Elicit answers, asking students to say which tense is used and why.

> **Answers**
> 1 *will not play* (future with *will*: negative future reference)
> 2 *became* (past simple: event in the definite past)
> 3 *has given* (present perfect: continues to be true in the present)

4 *welcomed* (past simple: event in the definite past)
5 *was climbing* (past continuous: interrupted continuous action)
6 *fights* (present simple: habitual present)

5 Ask students to use a similar range of tenses in their sentences.

6 Suggest students compare their sentences and tick the tenses used.

Reading

7 **KET Reading Part 4**

Ask students to look at the magazine photos, the title and opening sentence of the article and suggest what it will be about. Then give them ten minutes to answer the multiple-choice questions. Elicit answers and reactions to the article (which is a true story).

> **Answers**
> 1 C   2 A   3 B   4 A   5 B   6 C   7 B

8 Ask students to find examples of the different tenses.

> **Answers**
> | present simple: | *follows, has, think, email, keep, start, keeps, love* |
> |---|---|
> | present continuous: | *'s (still) living, 'm finding, is playing, 'm having* |
> | past simple: | *spoke, loved, took, heard, said, agreed, decided, didn't know, bought, learned* |
> | past continuous: | *was leaving* |
> | present perfect: | *'ve (only) been, hasn't changed* |
> | future with *will*: | *will come, 'll be* |

20.2 Lucky people

SB pages 124–125

1 Elicit possible reasons for the woman's expression and students' answers to the question.

2 Ask students to discuss where they will go and who they will take. Elicit answers round the class.

Listening

3   KET Listening Part 4

Play the recording twice and then elicit answers. Check spellings of 1, 3 and 4 and remind students that in 3, *Saturday* must have a capital letter.

Answers		
1 train/rail	3 Leyton	5 11.15
2 30(th)	4 Saturday	

Recording script

Ruth: Hello, this is Ruth Barnes. I've just heard I've won this month's radio competition!

Man: Ah yes. Congratulations.

Ruth: Thanks. What have I won?

Man: You're lucky, it's two return tickets to <u>Venice</u> from anywhere in Britain.

Ruth: I'll go with my mum. But is that by plane? She doesn't really like flying.

Man: No problem, they're <u>train tickets</u>.

Ruth: Great! When do we have to use them by?

Man: Well, you must travel before <u>30th</u> April, but today's only April 5th, so there's plenty of time.

Ruth: We can go during my school holidays. Will you send me the tickets?

Man: No, you must come to our office and sign for them.

Ruth: Where are you?

Man: The address is 47 <u>Leyton</u> Road. That's L-E-Y-T-O-N. It's near the theatre.

Ruth: When shall I come? I'll be at school tomorrow and Friday.

Man: <u>Saturday</u> morning, then. And you can have a look around the radio station if you'd like to.

Ruth: Great. What time? About ten thirty?

Man: Let's say <u>eleven fifteen</u>, then you can say hello to DJ Richard Rooster. His show finishes at eleven.

Ruth: I've always wanted to meet him. Thanks very much.

Man: No problem. We'll see you soon.

Pronunciation

4   Ask students to underline one word only in each question. Play the recording.

Answers
1 What have I <u>won</u>?
2 When do we have to <u>use</u> them by?
3 Will you <u>send</u> me the tickets?
4 Where <u>are</u> you?
5 When shall I <u>come</u>?
6 What <u>time</u>?

Speaking

5   KET Speaking Part 2

Explain that students should try to put suitable stress on one word in each question as they do the Part 2 task. Give them up to three minutes to complete each task and walk round listening to them, so that you can summarise any common errors on the board afterwards.

Vocabulary

6   KET Writing Part 6

Ask students to fill in the missing letters for each word. Elicit answers.

Answers		
1 special	3 single	5 happy
2 kind	4 clever	
The adjective in the yellow squares is *angry*.		

7   KET Reading Part 2

Check understanding of *millionaire*. Go through the exercise quickly, eliciting answers.

Answers
1 B   2 C   3 B   4 A   5 C   6 A

S pelling spot

Ask students to read the information before they do exercise 8.

8   This exercise can be set as homework if necessary.

Answers		
1 clock	3 booking, tickets	5 chicken
2 jacket	4 lucky	

Activity

Photocopy the KET 'money' on pages 131–132 of the Teacher's Book and cut it into notes. Make sure you have at least 30 x 1000 KETO notes and 20 x 2000 KETO notes (add more 1000 notes for a large class, see question 20 on page 107). Award the money suggested in brackets for a correct answer, take one 1000 note back for each wrong answer.

Millionaire quiz

1   Spell the name Scarlett Johansson. (1000 for each part of name)

2   Spell the plural of *sandwich*. (1000)

3   What is the opposite of *always*? (1000)

4   What is the past tense of *buy*? Spell it. (1000 + 1000 for spelling)

5 Name an animal that is found in Africa. (3000)

6 Spell the word *easiest*. (1000)

7 Name four words for clothes you wear outside. (1000 per word + 5000 bonus if all four are correctly spelled)

8 What do you say instead of *must* in the past tense? (2000)

9 Give examples of two future tenses. (1000 per tense)

10 Name four things found in a bedroom. (1000 per word + 1000 bonus for four)

11 Spell the *-ing* form of the verb *swim*. (2000)

12 Who is your father's brother to you? (3000)

13 What is the weather like today? (1000 for an adjective; 4000 for a longer response)

14 Spell the word *enough*. (3000)

15 What is the present perfect tense of the verb *find*? (2000)

16 Name four things that can travel on a road. (1000 per word + 1000 bonus for four)

17 Why do we have fridges? (up to 6000 according to the quality of the response)

18 Name four parts of the body. (1000 per word + 1000 bonus for four)

19 What language is spoken in Brazil? (1000)

20 Who is the most famous footballer today? (see below)

Allow the whole class to have an opinion on the most famous footballer and award 1000 to anyone who answers the question with a name + 3000 for a longer response, reason, etc.

E xtension activity

If students like the quiz, suggest they devise their own questions as a homework activity. Allocate a different unit in the course to each student and remind them to include questions on spelling as well as vocabulary and grammar.

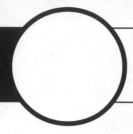

Units 17–20 Revision

This revision unit recycles the language and topics from Units 17–20, as well as providing exam practice for Reading Part 5 and Writing Part 9.

Speaking

1 Encourage students to give long and detailed answers.

Grammar

2 Give students a couple of minutes to write their sentences. Elicit answers round the class.

> **Possible answers**
> 1 If I buy a new mobile, I'll be able to send photos.
> 2 If I get a Saturday job, I'll earn some money.
> 3 If I become famous, I'll build a house with a pool.
> 4 If I eat more healthily, I'll feel better.
> 5 If I have a party, I'll invite all my friends.
> 6 If I do all my homework, I'll go out clubbing.
> 7 If I go on the internet, I'll visit some new websites.
> 8 If I take a break soon, I'll get a cup of coffee.

3

> **Answers**
> Martinique is the largest island *in* the area of the Eastern Caribbean. Over 300,000 people live *on* the island – many *in* the capital city, Fort-de-France. People speak French and it is taught *at/in* schools.
>
> The mountains on Martinique are old volcanos. The highest one is Mount Pelée, which is 1,397 metres high. *In* 1902, Mount Pelée erupted and about 30,000 people were killed.
>
> The weather *in* Martinique is warm and quite wet – perfect for the farmers to grow bananas *on* their land. Bananas from Martinique are sent all over the world, so look at the bananas *in* your fruit bowl. If they are from Martinique, they will have a blue sticker *on* them.

Vocabulary

4 There may be more than one correct answer.

> **Suggested answers**
> 1 robot (not to do with a computer)
> 2 back (not part of the face or head)
> 3 email (not posted)
> 4 Japanese (not European)
> 5 prize (the result, not what is done)
> 6 ready (not necessarily positive)

5

> **Answers**
> 1 B   2 A   3 C   4 B   5 A

Writing

6 Ask students to match the sentences to A or B. They could rewrite the two answers for homework.

> **Answers**
> A: 2, 5, 6
> B: 1, 3, 4

Reading Part 4

Questions 1–7

Read the article about learning Chinese.

For questions **1–7**, mark **A**, **B** or **C**.

LEARNING CHINESE

My name is Tanya, I'm American and I love learning languages. It all started when I was at school and I fell in love with Latin. I even spent time on a family holiday in Florida trying to understand how Latin verbs worked. Then I did Japanese, which was more enjoyable than Latin. But Chinese is the language I really love.

One day a friend told me about a new film. It was called 'A Chinese Ghost Story' and I saw it three times in four nights and decided to do a class in Chinese. I had classes twice a week for two years but didn't do very well because I am very bad at doing homework. I decided it was best to learn from someone who really knows the language. I asked a student in my class who comes from China to teach me. He and I often sat in parks and read stories in Chinese.

After that I went to Shanghai. I thought it best not to be with people who spoke English. But I had a terrible time trying to speak Chinese – even in shops and to the family I stayed with. The people who I talked to in Chinese were mainly aged six years old and younger. I think it was because I didn't have enough grammar and vocabulary! I kept trying but all the adults knew that their English was really better than my Chinese!

Example:

0 Tanya first learnt Latin

    A at school.

    B in Florida.

    C on holiday.

Answer: **0** [A ■] [B ☐] [C ☐]

---

1 Which language does Tanya like best?

    A Latin

    B Japanese

    C Chinese

2 Tanya decided to start learning Chinese after

    A talking to a friend.

    B seeing a film.

    C reading a story.

3 Tanya says she had problems learning Chinese because

    A she didn't work hard enough.

    B she wasn't given enough homework.

    C she didn't go to class often enough.

4 Why did Tanya like her second teacher?

    A He enjoyed teaching outside.

    B He was good at writing stories.

    C He was from China.

5 Why did Tanya go to Shanghai?

    A to study at a good school.

    B to practise her Chinese.

    C to teach English.

6 Who did Tanya speak Chinese to most in Shanghai?

    A people in shops

    B a Chinese family

    C small children

7 Tanya had problems speaking Chinese in Shanghai because

    A her Chinese was still not very good.

    B she didn't know many adults.

    C she easily got bored with trying.

Writing Part 7

Questions 1–10

Complete the cards.
Write ONE word for each space.

Example: | **0** | *in* |

> Dear Sam
>
> I'm sorry to hear you're (**0**) .... hospital. How (**1**)
> .... your leg feel now? You were lucky (**2**) ....
> to hurt anything else when you fell off your bike. I'd
> (**3**) .... to visit you soon. How (**4**) .... on Friday
> afternoon? When are you (**5**) .... to leave hospital?
>
> Love Helena

> Dear Helena
>
> My leg still hurts (**6**) .... it feels a bit better than
> yesterday. The doctor (**7**) .... I'll be home by Wednesday,
> so you (**8**) .... visit me there on Friday! Can you bring
> some (**9**) .... your DVDs? I know I'll (**10**) .... really
> bored at home!
>
> See you soon,
>
> Sam

Writing Part 9

You've just won a competition. Write an email to your English-speaking friend.

Say:

- **when** you heard about winning the competition
- **why** you decided to do the competition
- what **prize** you have won.

Write **25–35** words.

Listening Part 3

Listen to Patrick phoning Maria about the school play they are writing.

For questions **1–5**, tick (✓) **A**, **B** or **C**.
You will hear the conversation twice.

0 Patrick and Maria will meet to
talk about the play at

    A 4.00. ☐

    B 5.00. ☐

    C 6.00. ✓

---

1 Which folder on Maria's laptop
has the play in it?

    A the blue one ☐

    B the green one ☐

    C the red one ☐

2 Maria wants Patrick to work on

    A the beginning of the play. ☐

    B the middle of the play. ☐

    C the end of the play. ☐

3 Where must Patrick look for some
information about ice storms?

    A in a textbook ☐

    B on the internet ☐

    C in the library ☐

4 When does Maria want Patrick to
do everything by?

    A December 2 ☐

    B December 9 ☐

    C December 12 ☐

5 Whose home will they meet at?

    A Maria's ☐

    B Patrick's ☐

    C Tim's ☐

Test 5 Key

Reading Part 4

Answers

1 C   2 B   3 A   4 C   5 B   6 C   7 A

Writing Part 7

Answers

1 does
2 not
3 like / love
4 about
5 going
6 but
7 says/said/thinks/believes
8 can/could/must
9 of
10 be/get/feel

Writing Part 9

Sample answer

Hi Natalie

I've just had a phone call to say I've won a competition about Brad Pitt. He's my favourite actor, so I enjoyed doing the competition. My prize is an evening out with him and Jennifer Aniston!

Love,
Laura

Listening Part 3

Answers

1 B   2 C   3 B   4 A   5 C

Recording script

Listening Part 3

Listen to Patrick telling Maria about the school play they are writing. For questions 1 to 5, tick A, B or C. You will hear the conversation twice. Look at questions 1 to 5 now. You have 20 seconds.
Now listen to the conversation.

Patrick: Maria, I'm phoning about the school play. Can we meet at four o'clock to talk about it?

Maria: Sorry, Patrick, I'm in a Spanish class until five. I can see you after that, at six.

Patrick: Great. Before then, can you tell me which folder on your laptop has the play in it? I've looked in the red one, but it's empty.

Maria: It's in the green folder on the desktop. It's next to the blue one, which says 'Songs'.

Patrick: Right. Now, which part of the play do you want me to look at?

Maria: Well, I'm quite happy with the beginning, and Tim's helped me with the bit in the middle, but the play doesn't finish very well. Can you put in something funny there?

Patrick: I can try! Now, you want me to get some information about ice storms. Where shall I look?

Maria: See if there's a good website. I've tried the school library already and our geography textbook doesn't have anything.

Patrick: OK. Now, when do you want all this ready by?

Maria: Well, we're doing the play on December 12th and the last practice will be on the 9th. Can you get it to me by December 2nd, a week before that?

Patrick: Fine. Now, about meeting later. Shall I come to your apartment?

Maria: Why don't we meet at Tim's house? There's more space there than your flat or mine.

Patrick: Right. See you later, then.

Maria: Thanks, Patrick. Bye.

Now listen again.
(The recording is repeated.)

Key to Grammar folder exercises

1A

Answers
2 Can your sister come tomorrow?
3 Are Carmen and Maria from Brazil?
4 Do you like dogs?
5 Is it time to go?
6 Does Arturo catch the same bus?

1B

Answers
2 How do you get to school?
3 Where is your house?
4 What have you got in your bag?
5 Why are you angry?
6 Who does Ingrid know?

2

Answers
2 any   4 some   6 any   8 any
3 any   5 some   7 some

3

Answers
2 Does Pete really hate carrots?
3 Both Katie and Jack love chocolate.
4 My brother doesn't eat vegetables.
5 Rachel goes to restaurants three times a week.
6 Do you usually go to a party on New Year's Eve?
7 Supermarkets don't sell computers.

4

Answers
2 Did you enjoy the boat trip?
3 The coach didn't arrive back at school on time.
4 My mother made me some sandwiches to take on the trip.
5 We travelled to Rome by plane.
6 What did Lyn see when she went to New York?
7 He didn't speak Spanish at all on his holiday.
8 Where did she buy that souvenir?

5

Answers
2 but   4 and (but would also be possible)   6 or
3 because   5 Because

6

Answers
2 less expensive
3 the tallest
4 richer
5 sunnier
6 The most popular
7 the fastest
8 more expensive
9 better
10 the worst

7

Answers
2 was trying on; broke
3 was queuing; remembered
4 was choosing; went off
5 was studying; began
6 phoned; was having; left

8

Answers
2 may   3 must   4 can't   5 had to   6 can

9

Answers
2 are going to
3 will / 'll
4 am / 'm going to
5 will
6 will / 'll
7 is / 's going to
8 will
9 will
10 is / 's going to

10

Answers
2 Spanish is spoken in Peru.
3 The computer was invented by Charles Babbage.
4 The Harry Potter books were written by J. K. Rowling.
5 Presents are given on birthdays.
6 Spaghetti is eaten all over the world.
7 I was taught to swim by my father.
8 Chocolate is sold in sweet shops.
9 The World Cup was won by Brazil in 2002.
10 The car was stopped by the police.

11

Answers
2 swimming
3 choosing
4 using
5 sitting; watching
6 getting
7 running
8 driving

12

Answers
2 everything
3 Somebody/Someone
4 something
5 Everybody/Everyone
6 nobody / no one

13

Answers
2 It's too dry here to grow tomatoes.
3 The ice isn't thick enough to go skating.
4 The sun isn't hot enough to heat the water in the pool.
5 The fog is too thick to see the trees.
6 The wind was too strong to go sailing.

14

Answers
2 a large wooden reading desk
3 a popular American music magazine
4 an interesting adventure story
5 a friendly young detective
6 my favourite French comic book

15

Answers
2 Joan has just taken the customer's order.
3 Giorgio has just become a doctor.
4 Someone has just left a message for you.
5 I've just seen your mother crossing the street.
6 I've just spoken to the mechanic on the phone.

16

Answers
2 and 5   3 and 8   4 and 7

17

Answers
2 I turned on the radio to listen to the news.
3 I went to the museum to see an exhibition.
4 I borrowed some money to buy a CD.
5 I worked hard to pass the exam.
6 I bought a cake to take to the party.

18

Answers
2 If you eat an apple a day, you won't get ill.
3 If you don't eat too many sweets, you won't get fat.
4 You will / You'll lose weight if you stop eating snacks.
5 Your teeth will stay healthy if you visit the dentist regularly.
6 You will / You'll have bad dreams if you eat cheese in the evening.

19A

Answers
2 in   3 at   4 in   5 at   6 in/on

19B

Answers
2 on   3 at   4 in   5 on   6 in   7 at   8 in

20

Answers
2 has (just) made
3 is going out
4 ate
5 caught; was driving

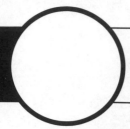

Photocopiable activities

1.1 Recording script

1

Maria: OK, Matt, let's start with you. What's your best friend called?

Matt: Er, Jonny, and he's thirteen, the same as me.

Maria: Right, and what do you do together, you know, in your free time?

Matt: That's easy to answer. We play football, as much as possible. We're in the same (**1**)_____, you see.

2

Maria: And Elena, what can you tell me about your best friend?

Elena: Well, her name's Raquel. Shall I spell that? It's R-A-Q-U-E-L.

Maria: Uh huh. And when do you get together? Like, just at weekends?

Elena: Oh no, we're best friends, Maria! I see Raquel every day … in school (**2**)_____, of course, and then we go out at weekends.

3

Maria: Kelly-Anne, I know your best friend is Vicky. And you see her every day?

Kelly-Anne: That's right, because Vicky's my sister.

Maria: Mmm, that's a really (**3**)_____ friend. So how old are you, Kelly-Anne?

Kelly-Anne: It's my birthday next week. I'll be fourteen … so I'm thirteen now.

4

Maria: Hi, Tom! Come here so I can ask you some questions. Who's your best friend?

Tom: My best friend … that's difficult. I mean, I've got lots of friends, but a best friend? I'd say it's Lucky, my (**4**)_____. You spell that L-U-C-K-Y.

Maria: Ah, that's sweet. So where do you go with Lucky? Do you take him for walks?

Tom: Of course, every day! We go to the river. Lucky likes the water!

Maria: Hope he can swim. OK, thanks, all you guys. See you.

All: Bye!

© Cambridge University Press, 2005

2.2 Number Bingo

1	4	9	15
16	18	20	26
28	35	43	47

1	4	10	12
14	17	21	26
30	38	42	45

3	5	11	15
17	22	24	27
34	41	46	50

3	7	8	16
18	23	25	31
39	40	46	47

2	8	10	13
19	24	27	29
30	33	36	45

2	6	10	11
14	18	23	32
39	48	49	50

1	5	6	8
12	13	16	25
37	40	44	49

3	4	6	12
17	24	28	29
31	38	43	50

© Cambridge University Press, 2005

3.2 Britain and ...

This information sheet is for British people who are going to live and work in your country.

Food

In the UK most people buy their food from large supermarkets. They usually do their food shopping once a week. They usually eat at home, but they sometimes eat out at Indian, Chinese or Italian restaurants.

My country

....
....
....

Holidays

British children usually have a summer holiday from the end of July to the beginning of September. Adults usually have four to five weeks' holiday a year. British people often have holidays in France, Spain or the USA. Camping is quite popular.

My country

....
....
....

School

In the UK children often go to nursery school at the age of 3 and then to primary school at 5. At 11 they go to a secondary school until they are 16. They can leave school at 16 or go on to do further study. Many children study French and German but they can stop at the age of 14!

My country

....
....
....

Transport

People in the UK usually travel by car. Not many people walk to school or work, or take a bus. The trains are quite expensive. British people drive on the left.

My country

....
....
....

Entertainment

Most British people watch five hours of TV every night. They sometimes go to the cinema. A lot of people enjoy shopping or playing on their computer.

My country

....
....
....

Sport

Football and rugby are the most popular sports in the UK. However, fishing on rivers and lakes is also popular. A lot of people go to sports centres where they can exercise in the gym and swim.

My country

....
....
....

Animals

British people like animals. They often have a pet – dogs, cats, rabbits and fish are very popular.

My country

....
....
....

Shops

Shops in the UK usually open at 9.00 am and close at 5.30 pm, Monday to Saturday. In large cities some shops are also open on a Sunday from 10.00 until 4.00 pm. In small towns there is sometimes a day in the week when the shops are closed for half a day. Shops don't usually close at lunchtime.

My country

....
....
....

4.2 Recording script

About two years ago I went with my class on our first school trip – five days in Paris! There were about thirty of us and four teachers. We all went in one big coach from our school in London. The teachers told us to be at school at four thirty in the morning. Everyone was there on time, but the coach didn't arrive until five o'clock and we didn't leave until five thirty! We were very cold and tired.

Anyway, the coach was very comfortable and we watched a video and listened to some CDs on the journey. We had some sandwiches and drinks with us so we went straight to Paris without stopping. The trip was quite expensive. It cost £240 and we wanted to save money so we didn't stop at motorway cafés. It only took us eight hours to reach Paris.

The name of the hotel in Paris was the Hotel Berri – that's B-E-double R-I. It was very old, but our room was nice and the bed was great – really soft! I shared the room with three other girls.

When we went shopping I tried to practise my French a few times but sometimes I didn't know the right words and spoke in English instead! The shops were great – I bought lots of presents, even a T-shirt for my little sister!

I think what I most enjoyed was the river trip. I took lots of photos of my friends and also of Notre Dame cathedral, and the wonderful art galleries.

I was sad to leave Paris. I had a lovely time there. We came home by coach and this time the journey was much shorter – we even arrived back half an hour early!

   © Cambridge University Press, 2005

5.1 Collocation Snap

do	take	make	spend	have
do	take	make	spend	have
do	take	make	spend	have
do	take	make	spend	have
homework	photographs	a cake	some money	a shower
homework	photographs	a cake	some money	a shower
a party	a cold	breakfast	a drink	a walk
a party	a cold	breakfast	a drink	a walk
a phone call	nothing	an appointment	time	a phone call
nothing	an appointment	time	homework	photographs
a cake	some money	a shower	a party	breakfast
a cold	a drink	a walk	a cake	a drink
do	take	spend	have	make
do	take	spend	have	make

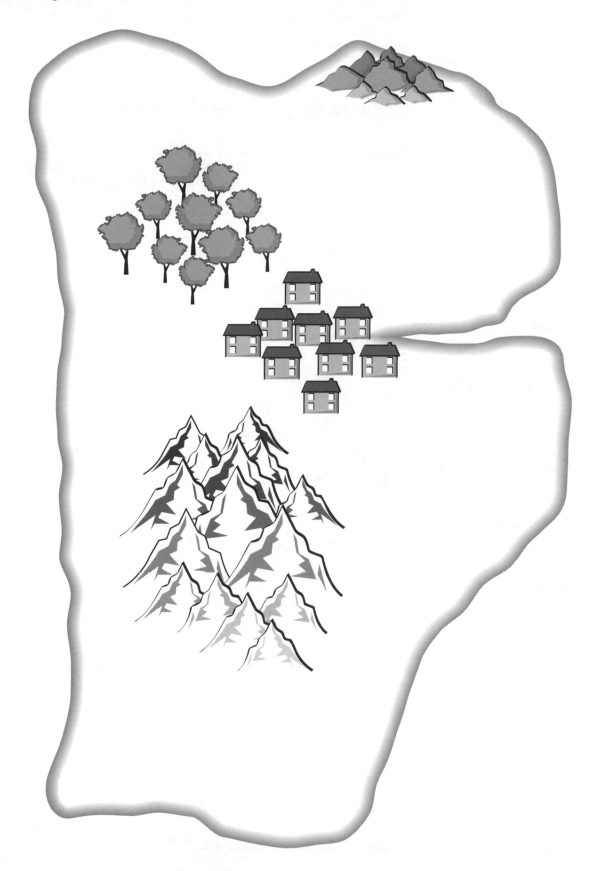

10.2 Activity

a wardrobe a chest of drawers	rice noodles	cola coffee
hamburgers hotdogs	cars cameras	Rolls Royce cars Ferrari cars
watches chocolate	diamonds gold	a bag shoes
a newspaper a magazine	a packet of biscuits a carton of juice	the English language the Hindi language
Romeo and Juliet Hamlet	bananas sugar	horses bicycles
a tie trousers	football basketball	my house Buckingham Palace

© Cambridge University Press, 2005

11.2 Recording script

This is the 24-hour information line for the Solway Fitness Club. Our opening hours are from six thirty in the morning until <u>eleven fifteen</u> at night, seven days a week. If you love exercising, you'll love our club!

We have a large gym with all the latest equipment. To book an introduction to the gym, please phone Jack Bergman on 0453 <u>88679</u> now.

There are two pools at the club. We have a ten-metre pool just for diving and a <u>twenty-five</u> metre swimming pool. Why not try relaxing in our steam room before you swim? It's fantastic!

If you'd like to become a member of Solway Fitness Club, please phone us again during working hours and ask to speak to Mrs <u>Colville</u>, that's C-O-L-V-I-double L-E.

We also give guided tours of the club once a week. These tours are at two fifteen every <u>Tuesday</u> afternoon. You don't have to book a place, but don't be late!

We hope you enjoy getting fit at Solway Fitness Club!

13.1 Recording script

Girl: How was your trip, Dan? I'd love to go round the world.

Dan: It was great. First we went to London, but only for a few days as it rained all the time. Both of us got really wet.

Girl: You went to Paris next, didn't you?

Dan: Well, Paris wasn't at all sunny but it was better than London – a bit cloudy.

Girl: Did you go up the Eiffel Tower?

Dan: Yes, we both had a great time!

Girl: Where did you go after Paris?

Dan: To Cairo. We saw the Pyramids.

Girl: Was it very hot?

Dan: It wasn't as hot as in summer. It was quite windy actually.

Girl: I'd love to go there.

Dan: Yes, you'd like it. We went to Sydney next. We didn't get to the famous Bondi Beach as there were a lot of thunderstorms. We did do some shopping there.

Girl: I bet that was expensive!

Dan: It wasn't as expensive as Tokyo. It was hot and sunny there – no rain at all for the whole five days we were there!

Girl: And then you went to the USA, didn't you?

Dan: Yes, to San Francisco, which is famous for its fog. It was so thick we couldn't even see the Golden Gate bridge! But it was warmer than some of the other places!

14.2 When do you say this?

1 **Start**	**2**	**3** Happy birthday!	**4**	**5**
6 Congratulations!	**7**	**8** What a pity!	**9** Speaking.	**10**
11 I'm just looking.	**12** Oh dear!	**13** It's Sue.	**14** Not at all!	**15**
16	**17** I've had enough, thank you.	**18** How do you do?	**19**	**20** Cheer up!
21 Have an aspirin.	**22** Never mind.	**23**	**24** Here I am.	**25** Me too!
26 Sorry?	**27** Excuse me!	**28** Can I try them on?	**29** How are you?	**30** **Finish**

15.1 Good and bad points

Job	Good points	Bad points

15.2 Recording script

Sam: Melody Music Shop?

Kate: Yes, this is Kate Richards. How can I help?

Sam: My name's Sam Bennett. I've just seen your advertisement for a Saturday job. What are the (1)_____?

Kate: The shop's open from ten to six but I need someone to start at nine and stay until seven. I'm always here from eight till eight on Saturdays so I really need help then!

Sam: I see. What kind of help?

Kate: Well, the (2)_____ is helping customers, being a shop assistant. I also want someone to do a bit of cleaning at the end of the day, so I can do the money.

Sam: Fine. How much do you pay?

Kate: If you aren't 18 (3)_____, it's £ 5.25 an hour.

Sam: Actually, I am 18.

Kate: Then it's £6.30, and after nine months I'll pay £7.00 an hour.

Sam: Sounds great! Er … where is the shop? I've never been there!

Kate: It's not in the town centre. If you know the university, it's about (4)_____ from there.

Sam: I live in Weston, but I can cycle along the river to get there.

Kate: That's true. Well, any other questions?

Sam: When can I come and see you about the job? I'm (5)_____ on Wednesday afternoon.

Kate: Sorry, I've got a meeting then. How about Thursday or Friday?

Sam: I can come early on Thursday, at nine?

Kate: Fine. See you then.

Sam: Great!

17.2 Recording script

Boy: Hi, Vanessa! Did you have a good weekend?

Vanessa: Great! I went to see a special James Bond exhibition at the Science Museum.

Boy: Sounds interesting, but I think museums are too expensive - I paid £8 last time I went.

Vanessa: This was only £6.50. I did buy a guidebook as well - that was an extra £2.95.

Boy: How did you get there?

Vanessa: You can take the underground, but I went by bus. It stops just outside. I got very tired walking around the museum though.

Boy: What did you see?

Vanessa: James Bond's helicopter, which was my favourite, and the tiny camera, and his car, things like that.

Boy: It sounds great! How early can you go in? At nine?

Vanessa: Not until ten, and we didn't get there until eleven thirty, so there wasn't enough time to see everything.

Boy: Can you eat there?

Vanessa: Yes. You can even take a picnic! I had a sandwich at a café but you can get a hot meal at the restaurant.

Boy: I'd really like to go. I'm free next Saturday - that's 23rd April.

Vanessa: The exhibition's on until the 27th, so the Saturday may be busy.

Boy: Well, I'll go on the 24th then.

18.2 How stressed are you?

1 **Start**	**2**	**3** Have you done your homework this week? Yes – Go to 20. No – Go back to Start.	**4**	**5**
6 Have you moved house this year? Yes – Move back 2. No – Move forward 3.	**7**	**8**	**9**	**10** Do you have problems sleeping? Yes – Go to 5. No – Go to 23.
11	**12**	**13** Do you eat too much chocolate? Yes – Move back 2. No – Move forward 5.	**14**	**15**
16	**17**	**18**	**19** Do you have a pet? Yes – Move forward 10. No – Move back 5.	**20**
21 Do you play a sport? Yes – Go to 40. No – Go back to Start.	**22**	**23**	**24**	**25** Do you watch TV more than 4 hours a day? Yes – Move back 10. No – Move forward 5.
26	**27** Do you bite your nails? Yes – Go to 12. No – Go to 32.	**28**	**29**	**30**
31	**32**	**33** Do you drink coffee or cola? Yes – Move back 5. No – Move forward 5.	**34**	**35**
36	**37** Do you buy clothes every week? Yes – Move back 5. No – Stay here.	**38**	**39**	**40**
41	**42**	**43**	**44** Are you a calm, happy person? Yes – Go to 49. No – Go to 34.	**45**
46 Do you have fun at least once a week? Yes – Move forward 3. No – Move back 2.	**47**	**48** Do you ever have negative thoughts? Yes – Move back 10. No – Move forward 2.	**49**	**50** **Finish**

    © Cambridge University Press, 2005

19.1 Recording script

Paul: Hello, Ruth.

Ruth: Hi, Paul. I (1) .... your fax at work this morning. Congratulations on the new job!

Paul: Thanks. I didn't have your email address with me, or Mario's, so I (2) .... to him on his mobile just now.

Ruth: Have you told Anna yet?

Paul: Well, I (3) .... a message on her answerphone but I think she's away. If I don't hear from her, I'll (4) .... her a text tomorrow.

Ruth: And what about your brother, Jack? He's away too, isn't he?

Paul: Yes, in Argentina. I emailed him from home this morning after I (5) .... the letter about the job. I know he'll be pleased.

Ruth: Was Tessa still in the flat when the post (6) ....?

Paul: No, but I've left a big note on the kitchen table for her.

Ruth: Remember to phone your professor and tell him.

Paul: I can't because the number at his university has (7) ....

Ruth: Oh, and he's no longer on email, is he?

Paul: It doesn't matter. I've already (8) .... him the news on a postcard. I bought one of that Moroccan carpet we saw at the museum.

Ruth: He'll like that.

SAMPLE

Candidate Name
If not already printed, write name
in CAPITALS and complete the
Candidate No. grid (in pencil).

Candidate Signature

Examination Title

Centre

Supervisor:
If the candidate is ABSENT or has WITHDRAWN shade here ▭

Centre No.

Candidate No.

Examination Details

0	0	0	0
1	1	1	1
2	2	2	2
3	3	3	3
4	4	4	4
5	5	5	5
6	6	6	6
7	7	7	7
8	8	8	8
9	9	9	9

KET Paper 1 Reading and Writing Candidate Answer Sheet

Instructions

Use a PENCIL (B or HB).
Rub out any answer you want to change with an eraser.

For **Parts 1, 2, 3, 4** and **5**:
Mark ONE letter for each question.
For example, if you think **C** is the right answer to the
question, mark your answer sheet like this:

0	A B C

Part 1

1	A B C D E F G H
2	A B C D E F G H
3	A B C D E F G H
4	A B C D E F G H
5	A B C D E F G H

Part 2

6	A B C
7	A B C
8	A B C
9	A B C
10	A B C

Part 3

11	A B C
12	A B C
13	A B C
14	A B C
15	A B C

16	A B C D E F G H
17	A B C D E F G H
18	A B C D E F G H
19	A B C D E F G H
20	A B C D E F G H

Part 4

21	A B C
22	A B C
23	A B C
24	A B C
25	A B C
26	A B C
27	A B C

Part 5

28	A B C
29	A B C
30	A B C
31	A B C
32	A B C
33	A B C
34	A B C
35	A B C

**Turn over for
Parts 6 - 9** ➡

For **Parts 6, 7 and 8:**

Write your answers in the spaces next to the numbers (36 to 55) like this:

0	example

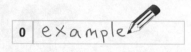

Part 6		Do not write here
36		1 36 0
37		1 37 0
38		1 38 0
39		1 39 0
40		1 40 0

Part 7		Do not write here
41		1 41 0
42		1 42 0
43		1 43 0
44		1 44 0
45		1 45 0
46		1 46 0
47		1 47 0
48		1 48 0
49		1 49 0
50		1 50 0

Part 8		Do not write here
51		1 51 0
52		1 52 0
53		1 53 0
54		1 54 0
55		1 55 0

Part 9 (Question 56): Write your answer below.

Do not write below (Examiner use only)
0   1   2   3   4   5

SAMPLE

Candidate Name
If not already printed, write name
in CAPITALS and complete the
Candidate No. grid (in pencil).

Candidate Signature

Examination Title

Centre

Supervisor:
If the candidate is ABSENT or has WITHDRAWN shade here

Centre No.

Candidate No.

Examination Details

0	0	0	0
1	1	1	1
2	2	2	2
3	3	3	3
4	4	4	4
5	5	5	5
6	6	6	6
7	7	7	7
8	8	8	8
9	9	9	9

KET Paper 2 Listening Candidate Answer Sheet

Instructions

Use a PENCIL (B or HB).

Rub out any answer you want to change with an eraser.

For **Parts 1, 2** and **3**:
Mark ONE letter for each question.
For example, if you think **C** is the right answer to the
question, mark your answer sheet like this:

| 0 | A B C |

Part 1

1	A B C
2	A B C
3	A B C
4	A B C
5	A B C

Part 2

6	A B C D E F G H
7	A B C D E F G H
8	A B C D E F G H
9	A B C D E F G H
10	A B C D E F G H

Part 3

11	A B C
12	A B C
13	A B C
14	A B C
15	A B C

For **Parts 4** and **5**:
Write your answers in the spaces next to the
numbers (16 to 25) like this:

| 0 | example |

Part 4

		Do not write here
16		1 16 0
17		1 17 0
18		1 18 0
19		1 19 0
20		1 20 0

Part 5

		Do not write here
21		1 21 0
22		1 22 0
23		1 23 0
24		1 24 0
25		1 25 0